I'M
GOING
THROUGH

▷ ▷ ▷ ► ► ► ►

DR. JERIS GRANT

Copyright © 2009 by JG Enterprise

ISBN 0-7414-4662-6

Published by:

1094 New DeHaven Street, Suite 100
West Conshohocken, PA 19428-2713
Info@buybooksontheweb.com
www.buybooksontheweb.com
Toll-free (877) BUY BOOK
Local Phone (610) 941-9999
Fax (610) 941-9959

Printed in the United States of America

Printed on Recycled Paper

Published February 2009

This book is dedicated to my mother, Beverly Grant Johnson and my grandfather, Johnnie Grant, Jr. for their untiring and continuous efforts, encouraging talks, and for teaching and showing me the greatest lesson—how to pray.

ACKNOWLEDGMENTS

I would like to first honor God, the father, Jesus, the son, and the Holy Ghost, for walking with me, for carrying me, for holding me, for molding me, for forgiving me, for restoring me, for keeping me in check, and for blessing me.

Thank you, Mama, for believing in your child, for sacrificing for your child, for wanting the best for your child, for doing the best to show your child the best. Thank you for your faith to smile when the lights or water was turned off. Thank you for letting your hair and nails be undone at times so I could go to ballet class, piano and violin class, showing me more. Thank you for your determination, your commitment to stand strong for yourself, your family and your community. Even you earned your Doctorate Degree in 2007! If any single parent wants to know how to go through, all they need to do is look at you.

Thank you, Granddaddy, for sharing your wisdom since I was a toddler. Thank you for seeing the good in bad, enough for me to know good from bad. Thank you for teaching me to "get off the floor;" for teaching me to "get an education" and for teaching me how to pray. Thank you for feeding my spirit scriptures and my body with that "good ole' Chinese food." When I wanted to give up, your words kept me from walking down the wrong path, one that I came close to traveling. My faith in myself grew wholeheartedly from your faith in me.

Thank you, Dad, for your efforts to be a great father. Our relationship is growing tremendously and I thank you for your contributions during my quest to be a thriving individual. Every time I had to move, which seemed to be never-ending, you were right there to help. We had good and bad times and

I'm glad we were able to push through the bad times. I truly appreciate your stepping in to help me reach my dream.

Thank you, Granny, for your many prayers and for being such a great inspiration to our family and me. There were times when I didn't know how I'd make it through. But you were right there and knew exactly how to contribute. I appreciate your graciously knowing when and what to do and I will forever be grateful to you for all that you have done.

I'd like to thank my best friends, Mia, Ndidi, Monique A., and KiKi for characterizing the word "friend" so well. Ya'll are the absolute best and I'm blessed to have each of you in my life.

There have been many individuals whom I've been privileged to meet and form encouraging relationships with at some point in my life, and I thank you for your roles. Thanks to Saundra Kirk, Denise Henley, Monique P., Nate S., and Nhan.

I'm sure my mom would join me in thanking Ms. Louise Scott, Ms. Paulette Wilkes, and JonnieMae for keeping and transporting me when I was little. I'm not sure if you all even know the word, "No". Thank you!

There was a gloomy day in January 2007 I thought was my last and there were angels sent to carry and encourage me when it seemed I was sinking in tears, literally falling to the floor and screaming from the pit of my lungs. I thank Midwife Reneau Diallo and Dr. Crystal Cash of Provident Hospital in Chicago, Illinois and Dr. Kathryn Burke of St. James Hospital of Olympia Fields, Illinois.

In all my traveling, I've been blessed to become a member and/or visitor at some of the best churches in the U.S.A. I make references to those Pastors in the book, and I thank you for accepting your call to preach the Word and lead people toward righteous, faithful and blessed living, which truly had an impact on my life.

I'd like to thank my entire family for your prayers, contributions, and presence.

A special thank you goes to Ms. Novella Ford and Family, Cousin Joyce Ferguson and Family, and Dr. Bridgette Smith and Family.

Thank you to all my friends, too many to name here, for all the great memories.

Thank you, Sorors of Alpha Kappa Alpha Sorority Inc. for being beautiful leading ladies of distinction.

Thank you to the teachers who educated me at Monte Sano Elementary School, Davidson Fine Arts Magnet School, A.R. Johnson Health Science and Engineering High School, Howard University, UCSD School of Medicine, New York College of Osteopathic Medicine, and New York Institute of Technology.

Thank you to the Family Medicine and Emergency Medicine Departmental Staff of Chicago College of Osteopathic Medicine.

INTRODUCTION

Every time a pastor mentions the common phrase, "When I look back over my life and think on how far I've come, I can't help but cry out to the Lord, Thank You," chills travel through my body as wonder turns into gratitude of how I made it through.

Every person that starts out in this journey called "life," no matter the ethnicity or the economic background, has a dream established during childhood. Every young adult has wondered at some point if that dream was so far-fetched, it might not become a reality. And every individual has experienced a difficult, stormy situation and contemplated what decision to make, which route to take.

When I first thought of my dream in middle school, I didn't have many resources or examples in my immediate vicinity to look upon for inspiration. I witnessed others with initially similar dreams eventually choose other paths, and I questioned what caused their change of heart. Then, as I sought after the dream, becoming the first physician in my family, I experienced first-hand some of the difficulties that might have triggered others to say, "Never mind that. It's just too hard."

This book not only gives references to some of the things that may hinder you from reaching your goal, your childhood dream, but it also sheds light on how to push through them. As you take a look at the Table of Contents, I'm sure you or someone you know will find some chapters to be a direct reflection of an event in your life.

When you attempt to climb the mountains of success, you should realize from the onset, that there is a method to arrive on top. I look at some television documentaries on mountain climbers and become both intrigued and inspired. They meticulously decide at which points on the mountain they will angle their sling for better grasping and which steps they will take. Many times they are climbing the mountains alone or with few others joining them, giving example that it doesn't take—and even more so, that you don't need—a crowd of people. They decide which cliffs are sufficient to rest upon for a few days and then they shortly get right back up to climbing. You see, when actually climbing a mountain, stopping points don't exist, resting points do. A mountain climber can't live mid-way on a mountain! It's either at the top or at the bottom, so still moments are rare. Sometimes they make the wrong step and fall downwards. They may even have to start over. The point is there is a sequence to reaching the top of a mountain.

I start the book with <u>Through Others' Opinions</u> because getting through what people think about you is fundamentally important and in many cases, is the initial hindering plight you must defeat. There will be those who are so intrigued by the size and magnitude of your mountain of success that they believe you can't climb that mountain no matter how hard you try. You must realize that no matter your past, no matter your environment, no matter your familial income, no matter what mistakes you've made, you have the potential to prove yourself beyond another's beliefs. Whether people are right or wrong about things that concern you, let their thoughts remain just thoughts. And let your passion be to prove them wrong.

If the negative thoughts of others happen to be true about you, you have the ability to change. How you start in this life is not necessarily how you will end. In fact, the objective of living should be in advancing from your start. Reaching your goals may indeed require you to change your habits, change your negative thoughts, change your attitude, and change your associations.

There are some things mountain climbers have to go through before they arrive and are able to look down at the mountain and around at all the beauties that being at the top of the mountain affords them to see. Likewise, there is a process in reaching your goal, getting through to make your dream a reality. There will be some still moments which you must get through; there will be sometimes when you get sick, feel ill or weak; there will be sometimes when your desire and faith is tested; and there will be sometimes when life's troubles can feel like an avalanche overcoming you. This book illustrates ways in which to overcome.

When you seek to reach the "impossible task," as some may refer to it, know there will be some distractions, some things that will seek to lead you off on a detour, and some things that will get you off track if you allow them to. Not only will you make some mistakes, but failing to recognize that you certainly made the mistakes is like turning a stumbling block into sinking sand. You may make mistakes in love, you may allow this love to rule you, or this love may actually become abusive. So, finding love or falling in love with someone too early may actually be a distraction. This book helps you identify your errors in love and life, and helps you take notice of ways to make your existence more enriching, despite the odds.

While dreaming is natural, actually choosing a career is difficult. And when you add to this discovering your purpose, you may soon start to see your life as a frustrating jigsaw puzzle. Deciding your adult path starts in your youth and regardless of the challenges that face getting a good and fair education, the obstacles are conquerable. When it comes to school, whether you refer to it as a "bookbag" or "backpack," typically it is full of educational books and supplies and should become the best friend that you never want to be seen without. It carries the essentials to your future and after all, your best friend should have your back, right?

When I sat down to pull all my thoughts and words to-gether for this book, I prayed before writing every chapter. I asked God to lead me. What He wanted to be delivered in this book, I specifically granted Him access, with the utmost welcoming. When I was asked to select a target audience, I admit to the initial difficulty, as I desired a book that would be beneficial to many demographics. It is my hope that you and someone you care about will be inspired at some point in the reading of this book and that it will serve as a timeless reference as you, too, go through.

▸ ▹ ▸▸I'M GOING THROUGH▸ ▹ ▸▸

TABLE OF CONTENTS

Chapter One

THROUGH
OTHERS' OPINIONS

"He that tilleth *his* land shall have plenty of bread;
but he that followeth after vain persons shall have poverty enough."
Proverbs 28:19.KJV

How is it so common for people to become victims of society? How is it so common and essentially easy for us to adjust to the perception of the world around us? As a teenager, I struggled with the thought of learning to become and stand firm as an individual, while simultaneously yielding to those around me and close to me, whom I considered my source of approval. Yet, teenagers aren't the only age group that struggle with obtaining and maintaining individuality. Even adults seek approval by their colleagues and peers and find themselves inevitably bound by the pleasures of others, not necessarily their own. Hard core gangsters struggle with individuality, having to conform to the organization's "way of life" in order to gain street credibility. And yes, even elderly people, as they plan death and funeral arrangements, consider what others will think of their casket and their program arrangement as though they will be around to receive the compliments! *"I wonder what they'll think,"* is such a familiar phrase. A phrase which although sounds at first caring of others, really inhibits a lifestyle of our own, for some even until death. It's

1

a phrase that naturally convicts all of us at some point. It's a phrase that prevents the birth of new idealism.

With almost every new task I entered, I had to endure difficulties that seemingly masked the task at hand. Being the first in my family to leave Georgia for college encountered negative thoughts by others that although accepted to Howard University, I would not *graduate* Howard University. Wanting to become the first physician in my family encountered the same sentiments summed up straightly by, "Yeah right, Jeris!" Though many times making me feel sad, if I allowed the thoughts of others to fully discourage me, I would not have accomplished much at all. It takes prayer and faith in a higher being, that being Jesus in my life, to get us through the negative perceptions of others around us. Otherwise, you will fail at your goal just because someone else "said so."

As a high school student I found that being different from some other classmates or trying to excel in science and math sometimes brought about empty feelings and those of not "fitting in." It is natural to evaluate yourself based on others. Unfortunately, it has also become natural to conform yourself to society. Evaluating yourself is one thing, but allowing those thoughts to guide your behavior and activity leads you down a path of losing yourself. Many of us on varying occasions have thought, "If I do 'A' he/she will think negatively. I don't want to upset anyone or feel misplaced. So I won't do 'A' even though it will help me grow and likely help someone else in the future. I'll *just* do 'B'. That way everyone will be happy." Wrong! While this may cross your mind, please do yourself at least one favor and do not follow through with the idea. Doing "A" because it's the right thing to do is one thing. But not doing "A" because you think it will please everyone is not realistic.

You have to realize that people and their opinions have little authority in your life. You must search yourself, pray, and follow in your desires, not necessarily to please others. Otherwise, you will find yourself consumed in a constant circle trying to please everyone, ignoring yourself. Pleasing others is something you may never really do anyway. It's never too late to realize this. But, it's better to understand it early in life because that's when we first seek to define ourselves based on others' opinions.

I remember feeling upset with what I saw when I asked a teenage patient what he wanted to do in life. Looking as if in concerned contemplation, he responded by shrugging his shoulders, while his mother replied for him shouting joyfully, "A football player!" Parents often force opinions of what they want their child to become, such as a doctor or taking over the family business. In this situation, I said to myself, "For goodness sake, the boy has a mind and interests of his own!" I couldn't help but feel hurt for the boy as I saw him feeling as though bound to fulfill his mother's dream, a thought no one should have to bear. I could see the disappointment he saw in his mother, if he decided to do something else in his life.

Parental guidance is important, of course. A child is far better with some sort of guidance than none at all. But parents should want more for their children, not necessarily for them to follow in their steps such as becoming a lawyer, professional ballplayer, or taking over the family business. Wanting more means letting children seek their own goals and God's purpose in their life. In order to succeed at your own dream and in order to build a legacy of your own by doing something different, you must first develop an attitude of "Who cares?" You may disappoint someone in the process of doing your own thing. But eventually the same person that you "hurt" may come around. If not, make sure you have been successful in reaching your goal. It is, after all, your life!

There are so many negative things in life to suggest that your goal cannot be achieved. As a student trying to build my application for medical school and go forward with my dream, I was firmly told by a medical school administrator while living in San Diego, "You will never become a physician." Following that, with an evil looking smirk he added, "I have no idea how that (physician) will happen." He patted my shoulder and offered two shallow words of advice, "Good luck." Please, if you can, try to imagine the sunken feeling I felt go through my body standing before him. Because I felt so strongly about my dream, I could have fallen to the floor! I tried so hard to stand tall, even though he made me feel so small. I respected him enough not to tell him where to shove his lyrics, while simultaneously remaining strong enough to hold back the tears while still in his presence. Those words from a person of earthly power hurt. I was absolutely devastated! And to describe a personal example of how others' opinions can convict, hurt and lead you to disaster, this was the time I thought about committing suicide. I didn't have a specific plan to accomplish it, but I sure had a thought. I told myself, if I cannot be a doctor, fulfill my dream to heal, I don't know what I'll do in life. I had no Plan B at that time. Plan B for me seemed to be an unfortunate, untimely, and self-induced death! Absolutely terrible! And not yet having any real financial independence of my own, my family and financial resources were stretched far and limited. So moving further into negativity brought upon by what some person said, as a need for money, I even contemplated working female escort services and performing exotic dancing!

This is a common Plan B that many women just happen to fall into! Young women of all ethnicities and economic backgrounds today have all heard the statement, "You gotta use what you have to get what you want." This does not mean using your brains, rather your body. Falling into this "choice" or trap of using your body is ultimately degrading, if you have a conscience. The Satanic forces some Christians like myself fight against know what we can be tempted with and just when the right moment is to "let the fan loose." Oh, how we can allow the opinions of others to completely change our path and alter our true destination!

As you can see, that man's opinion, his words, really hurt and threw me off track just a bit. Yet, when my strong-willed, single-parenting mom heard of his comments, and with her experience in educational social work, she became mad. While my scores were slightly sub-average, I was however, determined, presenting myself as a student trying to do better, trying to put forth a foot and excel. To hear that at a time when I was trying my hardest to be better and ultimately be best, definitely made me think to just give up. After nights crying with momentary beliefs in his statement, I had to be repeatedly encouraged by my mom and granddaddy. Referring to this demeaning man who bleeds as I do, I found strength to then ask, "Who is he?" He must have thought of himself seemingly as a God, powerful and all knowing of my future! I began to pray and did so constantly, "When others said I wouldn't, you [God] said I would. My fate is determined and I will be all that you [God] have intended for me to be, no matter who sees it, believes it, likes it, or not." As we say in the 'hood and around the block, "Forget what you heard! I'm gonna do the dog-on thang!" And, I did.

It's something to be said about people who don't care at all about what others think. Really! Driving in my old Hyde Park, Chicago, IL neighborhood one day, I saw this teenage boy who, in my opinion, truly looked a hot mess! Yet in his mind, he was being creative in how he dressed himself. His hair was cut in a Mohawk manner, shaved on both sides with a 3-inch Afro in the center. He had on cut up pants that obviously were two distinct black and brown patterns and at least two different materials sewn together! I had never seen two different materials, like wool and polyester, sewn together in a man's pants, or a woman's. He had on a ripped t-shirt, one sleeve long, the other sleeve cut off with the shredded ends trailing down his arm, ending with one hand wrapped in a green glove. Then his eye makeup! Yes, his bold eye makeup, obvious from across the street, consisted of dark circles around one eye, with the other having dark black lines forming the shape of sun rays. He had me wondering if I missed a parade or something! I realized it wasn't a costume when I saw him looking a similar hot mess a couple months later. But he was so confident and smiling, not caring that everyone in the cars nearby was staring at him from head to toe in complete awe! He didn't care! He really didn't care at all!

> I, even I, am he that comforteth you; who art thou,
> that thou shouldest be afraid of a man that shall die;
> and of the son of man which shall be made of grass.
> Isaiah 51:12.KJV

Let's take some time and really reflect on how it is people define themselves according to what someone else says. To help me in this, I remembered a book I read while in college in Washington, D.C., *Demian* by Hermann Hesse. In it, I read and quote, "People take things outside them for reality and never allow the world within to assert itself. An enlightened man has but one duty which is to seek the way to himself and discover his own identity." The author goes on to say, "People are afraid because they have never owned up to themselves...A whole society composed of men afraid of the unknown within them. To lose yourself is sin."

This author's words are quite deep so if you didn't feel them, please re-read his quote, as I would like it to really stick with you. There are a few things to gain from his statements. For one, take a look at how he refers to people as being scared of themselves. Now, if you're a violent person, you should be scared of yourself and the harm you can do! But let's relate this to different occasions, like to children and young adults growing up scared living in the 'hood, or in an environment not completely sustaining or fulfilling. They want more, but because of the foreseen difficulties in obtaining more, they become scared...scared to want more, thus scared of themselves. They want to get out of the 'hood, but because it's so hard, they become complacent, yield to the easy way, and feel afraid of wanting out or seeking something that they know within their heart is better for them, their family, or their legacy. We also become scared of being without welfare checks rather than without a job. No matter how unstable a job may be, it's better than nothing. Some people become scared of wanting a big house in a wealthy neighborhood, often filled with other races besides their own. Historically, we know people start to move out as soon as someone not like them moves in. We're not only concerned of what others think. We are a people scared of ourselves!!!

Secondly, the author tops it off by referring to how we sin when we lose ourselves. This is true! We hurt ourselves when we give up on our true desires and our "far-fetched" goals. We accomplish nothing for our children or ourselves when we let go of what's inside of us, that driving spirit. Suicide, another means of losing yourself, is a sin. And after all you go through on earth, why end life on a bad note caused by *you*? Seriously! Lastly, he refers to things outside us as being the reality. I have respect for people who care little about their bleak surroundings and things of the world, allowing their own ideas, dreams, and creations to rule them, which ultimately changes "the reality" in the world.

There was likely no greater degree of change in the world than in the early 1940s through the 1960s when the existence of slavery, separatism, and discrimination demanded disappearance. The people that lived during those years really wanted change, fought for it, despite how strenuous and hard the outside reality seemed. Now, it appears as though bringing about change is slow, as we have become accustomed to things as they are, yielding to

6

the dreams of others. I bounced back from a mistake of allowing words from someone else become a "reality" in my mind. When we have developed a dream and/or once we've started on a path towards a dream, we need to learn to stay grounded on our own two feet and to not be swayed when a teacher, guidance counselor, boss, friend, or family member disqualifies or does not encourage us. Stay grounded! See the way to yourself!

What people don't or may not want to see, God has already ordained! Thank God that the words people say are not factual. What people say is impossible has already been set up and arranged in the eyes of God. I hear so many students say, "I can't go to college because I don't have the money." My mom used to say to me, "Where there's a will, there's a way!" So, my answer in the form of a question to them is, "Have you heard of Financial Aid? Have you heard of work study or part-time jobs?" Their response usually is, "It's hard to work while in school!" And then I say, "Who said it would be easy? Do you want something that's easy or do you want something that will in the process enlighten you? Anything that's easily obtained is average. Do you want to be average or more than average?"

Everything is possible! For every excuse you find not to do something, someone else has found a different way to make it happen. You're only inhibited by your own mind and the negative thoughts of others you choose to let consume you. Don't get me wrong here, as funding higher education can be challenging. I attended a private medical school, which was more expensive than state medical schools. But in becoming a physician, if you are fortunate to go straight into medical school, without the extra time and money spent in graduate school prior to entry, most all expenses are covered with financial aid these days. Don't be afraid of a loan, but choose a career that will make paying for those loans easier.

When I think about costs, having some degree of debt can actually be a driving force. If I had sat down and actually calculated all costs prior to even thinking about becoming a physician, I would have given up with just the thought and not gone forth with the dream. Even in medical school, doing the math of how much it would cost me, at times, would give me a headache. I relieved the headache of costs in getting an education by thinking of my paycheck in the end! Of course, during schooling the thoughts of costs continued to cross my mind periodically, as any distraction would. But, at the end of the day, I had to think on the end result—that I would be a physician, a special type of physician, and able to pay back those loans.

The truth is, you cannot speculate on costs, as there are many options. The government even has some loan repayment programs available now for certain careers. There was no way I could predict that school administrators would raise tuition every year! And although I knew that eventually my financial aid would run out because of my expensive schools, I could not dwell on it until I actually had to face it. Even then, God made a way for me. When I couldn't afford rent, he provided me with rotations at hospitals that provided housing! When I couldn't afford food, living at dormitories that offered no cooking appliances, I found hospitals that provided food for free! Therefore, counting the dollars before you even approach the dream will only discourage and detour you. So many people fear finances, but even if you plan every dollar out to the penny and have it accounted for, there will still be something that comes up that was unknowingly considered. Faith will have you to take matters as they come, not into your own hands!

In a 1999 service at Metropolitan Baptist Church in Washington, D.C., Pastor Beacher Hicks delivered a lasting message to his congregation. He said, "While you plan to do, there are two groups that will always surround you. Those who do and those who won't. When you go to a new place that God sends you, you will be threatened by enemies. Nehemiah was a threat to the powers that be, but he was not controlled. People who do, don't concern themselves with people who won't." And then he illustrated this with what I call an "elevator function" of people riding up in an elevator. I believe not everyone wants, nor is fearless enough to go all the way to the top [floor]. Or we desire to go to the top, but some people are afraid of heights! Pastor said if the "won't do" people want to get off the elevator midway, they can do as they choose. So be it! But the "will-do" people have their package at the top and must not settle!

I thought about this long and hard and related it to the fact that sometimes people really can be an obvious hindrance, just existing in our lives as extra weight, creating a heavy load! Oh, how heavy elevators must get carrying all those "I'm going to settle" negative people! I speak for the elevator when I say stop wasting time just going along for the ride. If you're not really about it, go ahead and settle, get off! That dead weight is slowing down the elevator rise to the top! Why waste time getting up early for school, if you're not going to try to learn?! For those who desire to see what's on the top floor, know that no one is going to carry you there. How often do you see a doorman these days pushing the floor number for you? Doesn't happen! And the beauty of elevators is that there usually is more than one in a building. This means that there is more than one way to the top! If you find that there's too much dead weight slowing you down, get to another elevator. Find another way up without all the baggage! God has called us to be leaders, not followers. Push your own button. Make your own way! While you can encourage and help people to reach forward to the top or reach toward something new and different, you cannot force them to go all the way with you. You may not want to be at the top alone, but that extra baggage of people you may carry along could prevent you from fully reaching your true potential. You see, just to "belong" and be accepted with the clique, you may be tempted to get off on a lower floor, being less than your true potential. Learn to "Drop Off" (the clique) because trust me, you don't really want to join the "I could have club."

It takes a very strong and focused person to continue to hang around a bunch of people who deserve more, but desire less. Popular belief tells us, "One bad apple spoils a bunch!" But I like to think of it as, "A bunch of bad apples can spoil a perfectly good one!" Some of those people you're hanging with, you've got to drop them off! Those negative thoughts you've adapted from others and become so accustomed to, you've got to drop them off, too!

Accepting less, leads you to falsely believe that you will not have to prove your case or answer so many questions for wanting something higher. Unfortunately, because there are more people living *beneath* their goal than *at* their goal, you misbelieve that you will be surrounded by people with desires like you. Truth is, you will always have to answer to people for not conforming, or answer to yourself for conforming. Either way, you'll have to answer. If you choose to conform, you will have to do it over and over again in order to maintain your "likeability." So, let me challenge you to let God prove your case. Stand on faith. Be glad that you don't have to be with the clique. My granddad once told me firmly, "You don't have to convince no one! Let God handle it. And you will understand it by and by. Remember, God is in control." If you expect to receive a reward from others for following their wishes, think again!

For everything that occurs in our lives, there is an answer in the Word of God. When I think of someone who overcame the ultimate of others' opinions, I can't help but refer to Jabez. Some people think there's a lot in a name. Jabez didn't! Yet, naming today can be comparable to a complicated calculus math equation, as parents-to-be spend so much time figuring out a name for their newborn. Whether it's combining the mother and father's name to create a name for the child or using some adjective to name him/her, it can all be a tedious, imaginative process that may make a ridiculously sounding name. Even I had no idea that my name wasn't some new creation, slightly altered from someone else's name, until I met a middle-aged patient while living in Buffalo, New York, who was a native of Sudan that shared my name. It was a bit weird, seeing her name on the patient list. I had to take a double look! The other doctors told me that I wasn't just seeing things. In broken English the patient described, "Jerisa means with God, you have everything you want." I thought, "Wow, how cool is *that*!" She is from Sudan, has my name, and it actually means *something*! But, with all the names we create these days for our descendents, none can compare to the meaning of Jabez, whose own mother gave him a permanent staple of how she bore him in pain! Oh, what it must have been like to grow up knowing the hatred of the one who carried you for nine months.

Many fostered and adopted children experience similar modes of hatred, which may indeed be an act of love, when they think of their separation from their birth parents. But, 1 Chronicles Chapter 4 tells us that in spite of Jabez's name, in spite of the action by his mom, Jabez turned out to be more honorable than his brethren! Now, really, how cool *is* that? Instead of relying on mommy or daddy's judgments, Jabez cried out to God and did not wallow in the negativities of his birth. He cared about no one else's opinion and knew exactly what to pray for. He prayed against his own name, for goodness sake! And with that prayer, all that his mother intended for him to be, to cause pain, had no place in the hand of God.

Plainly, it does not matter what other people have for you to do, what other people call you, or what other people say you can't do! What gets you through their opinions is prayer to the One who is above everyone! Learn to reject the negative thoughts of others and move forward in faith of what God, not man, can do. Say to yourself as the scripture tells us, "If God be for me, who can be against me? Who shall lay anything to the charge of God's elect? It is God that justifieth." With God, no one can jump on you and tear you down or else they should know what they're dealing with. The battle is not yours. You're not in it by yourself. Jabez was blessed simply because he refused to let any obstacle, person, or opinion loom larger than God's nature. Likewise, God has placed you higher than any opinion! And there is no opinion greater than prayer and God's plan!

This is easier said than done, however. But after being hurt by enough people, after being misunderstood by enough people, you will learn to ignore opinions and be glad when someone misjudges you, be glad when someone misclassifies you, or be glad when someone negates your abilities. As long as you're grounded in yourself, their miscalculation of you will be their issue, not yours! Even though you really have nothing to prove, you've got to get happy "proving" people wrong. When you get ready to do something different, whether it's considering your own business, losing weight, or becoming an A-student, there is no doubt someone will have something to say.

> And whosoever shall not receive you, nor hear you,
> when ye depart thence, shake off the dust under
> your feet for a testimony against them.
> Mark 6:11.KJV

When I contemplated medical school, I heard indirectly from one woman who was unable to convince her child to be a physician, "Why on earth do *you* want to be doctor? Augusta doesn't need any more black doctors." In my mind, my answer to her was, "How do you know I want to live in Augusta and who made you a census interpreter and representative of blacks in the city?" Then I heard she would also say, "Doctors don't make any money. It's a waste of time." My thought to that was, "Different types of doctors earn different profits. How do you know which I shall be and they all make at least 3 times what you make so what are you talking?" My point is, you have to develop a backbone and be ready to expect, to embrace, and then kick the mess out of criticism with your own response. Out of respect for the elderly, I never told this person my real thoughts. I didn't have anything to prove to her verbally. If she doesn't get it, she just doesn't, and likely never will. I just needed to fix my mind with the reality of the situation. My mom has a favorite poem by Edgar A. Guest that she spoke over and over again while I was growing up. I must have committed it to memory in my pre-teenage years. It begins like this, "Somebody said that it couldn't be done, but he wouldn't say so until he tried…and soon what others said he couldn't do, he had done it!" As they say, "Make your haters your motivators".

I would like to believe that comparing yourself to others helps you in the end. Really, I would! But honey, there is no such thing as equal talents! So, no matter how hard you try to be like someone else, it will never happen. Their dream is simply theirs! You must not look on the esteem of others as being the renewal of excellence, because often you will see the opposite. What is excellent for them will be corrupt for you! And what you think is excellent for them, may not even be that at all behind their closed doors. Don't live your life in accordance with the "copy cat" theory. Thinking, "She did it, so I think I can do the same thing, too" doesn't work for long. And, why do you want to master someone else's dream anyway? When did becoming a "copy cat" be the thing to do? Get your own thing going. But, in the process, be open to critiquing yourself. If you sing like a howl, you can't compare yourself to the greatest of all singers! Obviously, your talent is not to sing. Instead, maybe it's for you to *write* eloquent songs. If you can't rap, produce rap music instead. You don't have to be on the frontline in order to fulfill your purpose!

When I was just beginning medical school, I remember when I was selected to become a prospective model in this talent and model search. Naturally, girlfriend [me] was beyond excitement! But, here I am, having worked so hard to get into medical school, now getting ready to fly after another idea just because some people tell me, "You can be a model." It was a worthless conclusion that was soon followed with, "But you have to pay money for it to happen." I'd have to pay a lot of my own money to get started and thus learned that I had not *really* been selected! Being pretty did not make me a model although they wanted me to chase their idea. If I hadn't come down with a mild, but extended form of Pityriasis Rosea (non-contagious skin rash), I might have been on pins and needles trying to collect funds for something I was not meant to do! Contrarily, I was told by several men that because of my "sexiness" in their opinion, I didn't *look* like a doctor. I remember being at a house party in Chicago when this guy questioned my friend after she told him I was a physician. He said to her, "No way. Not her." Just because you have a nice body doesn't mean you're supposed to be a centerfold in a magazine. I didn't know whether to take that as a compliment or as an insult. Nonetheless, every door that opens is not for you. Don't knock on every door that exists, as it could be a trick, especially if you're already on a path that you desire! And comparing yourself to others, thinking you're something that you are definitely not, will lead you to a door that ultimately slaps you in the face! Pow!

God is weary of having to lead around people who he has to issue commands to repeatedly. It is better to have not heard than to disobey. If you pray for a purpose, as I hope you will, and when this purpose is confirmed, do not question that purpose and seek approval from others for this is a form of disobedience. So many of us take the scripture referring to someone seeking counsel from the wise to an entirely different level as though everyone they consult will come up with the same "wise" conclusion. How many people does it take to verify God? Really, how many!?

Ndidi, one of my best friend's favorite scripture is Proverbs 19:21 which says, "There are many devices in a man's heart; nevertheless the counsel of the Lord, that shall stand." Be very cautious in receiving a multitude of advice from people so you do not feel bound to please them. Besides, too much advice is altogether confusing, don't you think? As you search for success, knowing who you are, to whom you belong and taking advantage of those silent moments with God are the final things you need to keep His opinion higher than those of others. Do not be afraid to do something new or something that the world may say is difficult for you to do. Do not get discouraged when you are misunderstood.

Don't be afraid of yourself! Just because you didn't own up to yourself and your reality once in your life, doesn't mean you can never do it. Let negative opinions be a foundation to achieve greatness. And while you desire to be liked, loved and respected by all, don't be a slave to people!

Chapter Two

THROUGH
THE STILLNESS

▷ ▶ ▷ ▶ ▶ ▶ ▶

A major question we face in life, often more than once, is when to be still versus when to make a move. Many people struggle with this concept of stillness. While seeking their goal or purpose, some people appropriately take a break, maybe for self-evaluation. Others, inappropriately take a break, an extended one at that, and attempt to justify the break as a time to just "stand still". I remember becoming captivated during my last year of medical school, watching a turtle while vacationing with my mom at Amelia Island, Florida. One morning from our deck, my eyes drifted from the ocean view and fell upon this turtle that was traveling in the sand. I would look away briefly, but then return my eyes many times to see the very *same* turtle. This happened a few times and then I realized that the turtle was actually in the *same* place! Although it seemed to be moving, the movements were so slowly paced that I just knew I could never lose sight of him! I'm sure the slow movements had to be coupled with numerous breaks as it seemed the turtle had gone absolutely no where! Sometimes, I even wondered if it was even alive! Eventually, although enjoying nature, I got tired of looking at this sluggish-moving turtle, so I again focused my attention on the ocean. Testing my hypothesis that the turtle was hopeless, I once more fixated my eyes on the location where it had been and to my surprise, it was gone!

You see turtles, unlike many of us, are slow moving, cautious animals who know exactly where they are going and will creep on until they arrive. You may think they're not going anywhere, taking their sweet little time, but when you least expect it, they are out of sight and out of mind, handling their business. People, on the other hand, can be so slowly moving until we reach a stand still! You look away and return noticing that some people are still in the same place. Nothing has changed. Some graciously characterize it as a break point. Either way you describe it, many of us become stale and locked into a so-called "comfort zone". Thus, many of us never retrieve the momentum we started with and therefore, never arrive at our purpose or achieve the "impossible".

> The Lord is good unto them that wait for him,
> to the soul that seeketh him. It is good that a man
> should both hope and quietly wait for the salvation of the Lord.
> Lamentations 3:25-26.KJV

This scripture, along with Psalm 46:10 and its directions of one waiting and being still, has become more than a word to stand on, but a welcomed self-restriction that many rely on as excuses not to act. I believe there is a time to stand still and a time to move about on faith. Yes, we should do as Exodus tells us, "Stand still and watch the works of the Lord". But, we should also do as Hebrews tells us, "Cast not away therefore your confidence, which has great recompense of reward." We must realize when to stand still and when God is telling us to make moves, to work. Our Daily Word Magazine said it best with, "Pray as if everything depends on God, work as if everything depends on you." I believe you must be careful how you just stand, as you could indeed fall.

Many people think they have nothing to lose if they don't make a move. Wrong! Realize that you can actually be standing still, without making a move, and still fall (or fail). You might ask, "How is it possible that I fall (or fail) if I don't make a move, if I just stand still?" Well, let's look at a literal example for a moment. Have you ever tried standing up straight, being still, without moving? Try it now for as long as you can. When I did this, my legs became weak and tired. I had to rotate the weight bearing of my legs so I wouldn't lose balance...and then, FALL flat on the floor! In order to keep from falling, I would either need to take a step with my right or left leg, choosing which one was a risk, but one that must be made in order to find some sort of bodily relief. I even got anxious, tired, and bored just standing there! I said to myself, taking a move, doing something, has to be better than what I'm doing now...nothing!

Often, when I worried about something or didn't know what action to take, my mom told me, "Jeris, just stand still." And when I did not do this, regretting my action, she would of course remind me by saying, "I told you to just stand still." Many times, when we're on the verge of making a decision or move, we get frequent reminders of how we should stand still. We hear someone say, "Now you *know* you're not supposed to do that!" On the contrary, some people are walking around doing things and saying, "God told me to do *this*." Well, God might not have told them anything! In reality, that could be their way of confirming themselves. So yes, we could even be making plenty of moves, yet pointless ones, becoming busybodies, really accomplishing nothing at all. Realize these are the moments we *should* stop and be still.

Knowing when to stand still can be difficult, if you make it that way. I found more reminders to be still than those to make moves, to take risks. So, I choose not to answer your questions on when to be still, but to offer you hope in getting through the still moments and all of its possessions you've so readily adapted to. Being still can be quite easy, not requiring much energy at all. But, getting out of the comfort zone and from underneath the same radar is where many of us need encouragement. It is possible for you to become undetectable, as my Florida turtle did. You can reach heights deemed unattainable. But, you must not be still too long!

I speak with people who respond to their action as, "I'm just standing still." My question to them is, "For how long do you plan to just stand still?" I mean, you catch up with them in three years, and they're still "standing still"! Really, what reason *are* you still standing there? Others respond to their action as "I'm just waiting on God." Or some will say, "Look, I'm moving at my own pace." My replies are, "Well, have you ever thought that God might be waiting on you? And then, have you ever thought about picking up your pace because it's nearing zero, honey!" Getting through the stillness includes communing with the Lord, aligning wholeheartedly with him for discernment so you'll know, *that* you know, you are supposed to move or to continue standing still.

The only temptation that has come to you
is that which everyone has.
But you can trust God, who will not permit you
to be tempted more than you can stand.
But when you are tempted, he will also give you a way to
escape so that you will be able to stand it.
1 Corinthians 10:13.KJV

The first step you should take in order to get through your complacency is realizing you are going to make mistakes. This way, you won't be disappointed with the mistakes you inevitably will make. In order for you to be perfect, you'd really have to be alienated or removed from the world. We strive for perfection, but no one *is* perfect. Some people are so panicky of making a mistake. Goodness gracious! I'll never forget someone I knew who adamantly believed he could not make mistakes, and was so convicted to stay still until seemingly God himself, came to his town, took him by the hand and led him. Even if he in some way perceived what he was supposed to do, he would not believe it, and stood still again, so as "not to make a mistake." In his mind, it was impossible for him to make a mistake because as he said, "God doesn't make mistakes!" I said, "Of course God doesn't, he's God! You're not! True, you're made in His image, to be like Him, but you ain't God."

Early in my spiritual quest, I realized that there are two forces in this world. Stepping out of the stillness, you will be tempted. Something is seriously wrong if you're not. You may fall. But you must know that if you fall, you can get up. If you don't realize first that you may fall, you won't know that you can get up. Thus, you'll stay down. Don't give yourself a stomach ulcer trying not to make mistakes. I heard it stated once, "Some people are so spiritually grounded that they're no earthly good." You must know both the spirit *and* when to act in the natural, being spiritually guided. Faith is a substance, in my mind, to be relied upon *and* acted on. We all fall short sometimes. But life goes on and so we must too. Don't allow your fear of making mistakes lead you into self-made confusion and another standstill.

Making mistakes is one fear you must get over, but it can also be a light way to phrase our common acceptance of stillness. For some, it really becomes a matter of us not stepping out on faith. Yep, that's right! It's not that we're only afraid of making a mistake each time, but that we can't let go and let God. Revitalize yourself into the faith zone! In regards to faith, there is a difference between faith *in* God and faith *of* God. I heard it described once as, "Faith *in* God will *allow* you to do great exploits, but the faith *of* God will *enable you* to command that a mountain be moved and it will. Faith *of* God says that what cannot be seen and done is already done." I believe there is a progression and trial of your faith!

Contrary to popular belief, faith is not a static concept! It is not the "substance" that we should just forever stand still on. It is not good for you to just "have faith," as faith is not complete or whole without movement. How is your faith justified if you never make a move? Because of your stillness, in many instances you're not really being faithful. What you're doing instead is standing in a "safety zone" with God, and in a comfort zone with your mind. God moves! If you have the faith *of* God, you'll know when to move, too. And he calls you to fight so make your move *by* faith!

Sometimes, we are still not because of unforeseen mistakes, or that we're faithless, but because we are simply scared and afraid. Most men will never admit to this, but their high level of testosterone doesn't exempt them from fear. This is critical to understanding still moments. A little fear is acceptable and goes along with thoughts of taking risks. Fear is an appropriate response. If I became a little fearful of something, my mom would ask me, "Hasn't God proven himself to you time and time again?" And I would say, "Yes, but." Then she would cut me off with, "No buts, Jeris." Out of all the excuses we find to be still, being scared is the only one I will agree to, but only for a short time. We must get over our fear of taking risks and just take them. I got over many fears by switching my thoughts to those of the benefits gained once the task is accomplished. It works! For example, there are plenty of risks in deciding to start a business. But, instead of staying still because of the fear of failure, think of how good it would be to be your own boss. Think of how good it would be to make your own schedule. Think of how good it would be to decide your own income potential. Or think of how your business could help someone else. Benefit-thinking can outweigh the fears of taking risks! Changing your thoughts to all things positive will get you through those still moments caused by fear. Remember, you can fail while doing nothing. Try fearing being in the same place if you don't take risks.

Many people believe in God, have faith *in* God, but don't believe in themselves. By saying believe in yourself, I'm not referring to believing in your qualifications or lack thereof. I mean simply believing that you can do "it," whatever "it" is in your life. Whether you're in your youth starting out on a dream, or in your adulthood, seeking transformation of some sort, you have to believe in your worthiness to achieve the impossible.

There is a shoeless, homeless lady who walked in the rain in San Diego that I mention in this book a few times. I've seen homeless people in distress and have actually been homeless and frustrated myself. Yet, it was something about this lady that made her look too comfortable walking the streets barefoot. Yes, she was determined to get to wherever she was going regardless of the weather and road conditions. But, I wondered if it became commonplace for her. I wondered what episode really caused her to accept this stillness in her life? I had to live in my car a few days while also living in San Diego. I slept in the garage of a grocery store. The hard part was that I was working at night, and so trying to sleep in a busy grocery store garage was not a great way to rest. I'm sure some people had to wonder what I was doing wrapped up in the back seat of my car, looking as though I was really comfortable getting that sort of sleep. But, it was not comfortable. Yes, it's a joy to simply see another day. But, it was not a joy being crumbled up in the back seat of a car for days on end!

If we can first ask ourselves, "Is there a better way," and if we can then believe that *there is* a better way, we can move on a path *towards* that better way. Forget the barriers right now! First, believe there is better! I am not attempting to make this sound simplistic as many do face hard times filled with struggles. So, before you say sarcastically, "Yeah right, Jeris, everything will be great if I only believe;" let me encourage you that even when there is a huge stumbling block before you, as many minorities face, you must still first believe. You have to start with something, right? Stop doubting yourself! Believe there's a better job. Believe you can be healthy in weight. If your family can't afford higher education, believe in better grades for scholarships and/or financial aid. If you don't get a scholarship, believe you will be able to repay loans. Believe the best for your children, if not for yourself. Believe you can have *"that thing"* in spite of your family background. And even if you're on your deathbed, die believing in the life you lived. We all know that even rich people are not always happy. So, you can actually have everything, but if you don't believe in *"that thing,"* it will not happen. And this, believe me, is *that* simple!

James 21:2(KJV) tells us, "You have not because you ask not." We also have not because we *act* not. But, in our inquiries, we can get sidetracked as to whom to ask about what steps to take. Once you have decided to believe in yourself, not in your abilities, of course the next step, at least for me, is to ask God for guidance. Some of us like to ask a bunch of other people what we should do with our lives. But when I do this, I end up more confused and lost than before I asked anyone! Everyone has something different to say! I found that God does order your steps when you ask Him, better than anyone else. So, ask God! For me, there was no greater stillness of a time than my stay in San Diego. Even with all of my praying to get into a good medical program that offers me exactly what I need, the prayer alone wasn't enough. For me, it took some movement of faith, I believe, just to let God know that I was in this with Him. Now, some religious folks just read that and are responding to it as, "God doesn't need any help, missy." Know that I'm not implying He does. But, whether it was a sacrificial gift at church or a sacrificial gift to a stranger, for me, I had to do something in addition to my asking. For you, it may be giving up a lifestyle that you know has been dangerous, or leaving that "false" love that hurts you daily in order to really receive what you asked for, the "real" love. Put your "money" where your mouth is. You're asking God to do this and that, but what are *you* willing to give up? Give God all or nothing. Many of you are choosing to give Him nothing.

When you ask God faithfully, with both your resolves to do and not to do, he will answer and order your steps. But what I've noticed is that even after God has given you the answer, many of you still choose to do nothing but stand still. This shows that you doubt God, even though you may believe in yourself. So, we fail to listen where God speaks. Hello! Can you hear Him? Your prayer has been answered! Yet, you choose your own way or choose to stay standing still. And furthermore, you think this "endurance" to stand still will lead you to all things perfect! Wrong! In this circumstance, you're not standing still. You're in denial! And denial will cause people to miss their true blessing. Yes, you *can* miss your blessing.

I learned that blessings will make room for themselves, but I haven't always known that. I myself, would question, "Did God do that?" And then answer my own question, "No, he couldn't possibly because I don't deserve that. Could this *really* be?" And I've known others to pray upon a scripture, receive an answer and then decide to pray on another scripture, never making any moves! Even some religious people will keep finding new scriptures for them to lean on, when God has clearly given them an answer a long time ago. You're in a cycle of finding scripture after scripture to lean on, going in a cycle, seemingly never exiting a circle. Many religious people believe it is impossible to miss your blessing. But, I believe many of us, if not on the verge of receiving a blessing, have a blessing right at hand and deny it. Wake up! Even Deuteronomy 28 begins with an "If"! So, although we really don't want to, yes, we can miss our blessing. It is God's will that is working in you to give you the courage, power, and strength to do His purpose. His will is in you, but He can't MAKE you take a step. *You* have to do that part. Don't think too much into an activity, creating your own jigsaw puzzle. God can show you the way, but you have to choose to move. You should seek to know when to get up and move to claim your blessing before it passes you by. Stop waiting on God alone and *do* something!

I've always wanted to learn how to play the game of chess. I would hear of a chess tournament on television and think, "How unique is that!" Watching the players take time to study the board with each new game as though they had never seen it before was quite interesting. Some players would just take forever deciding what move to make and I would say, "C'mon already, is it really that serious? You're wasting time. Make your play!" Even golfers incur a delay, taking some time to study "the green" and the relationship of the wind and how it will affect their move.

Think about it, if chess and golf players do not make a move, they forfeit the game! But when they finally decide to make a move, they do it for the right reasons. Taking your time is an understood instruction during these types of games. But, you only have so much time to be still. Then, as in the game of life, you've got to make a move. Time isn't going to wait for you forever. So do it now!

My grandfather used to quote a poem that I love. Although never finding the author, the poem simply states, "If a task is once begun, never leave it until it's done. Be the labor great or small, do it well or not at all." Once you've decided to make some sort of move towards your goal, hopefully one led by prayer, know that giving up is not an option! If you reach a difficult class, don't keep changing your major! You'll never graduate that way! Fight on until you put that hard class behind you. I mean, you *know* how complicated it was to get you to finally *make* a move? So don't quit now that you've gotten past the most difficult step! Giving up was a thought that crossed my mind many times, mostly as I traveled for hospital rotations during my junior and senior years of medical school. Driving on various highways, packing up, moving here, and unloading there, led me to the point a few times where I never wanted to see a highway again! I asked myself, "Is it really worth all of this?"

The longest trip I've driven was a 14-hour one, but it was during the 12-hour one from my home town to Allentown, PA where breaks and rest stops became commonplace. Driving through western Virginia and Pennsylvania, I distinctly remember my car swerving from side to side because of the strong winds. So, I thought to take a few breaks. But, I realized that many times when we think to take time off, we simultaneously think of when or if we'll restart again. Although I really hadn't been driving that long, I wondered if I would stop and rest for just a few minutes, or get a hotel and stay the night. And staying the night this time would not have been a good decision. Those mountainous winds shook me for a moment, moving me to the point of really wanting to rest. But, I realized that I had already missed two days from this new hospital rotation because of a conflict in a scheduling sequence with another hospital. As a result, I decided to hold on tight and push on, for had I taken that break at that moment, I might not have wanted to start back on my route, with that weather.

Sometimes we think of taking breaks just because we think there will come a better time to continue on the path. Not necessarily so! These are the breaks that lead to wasted time and what we really should do is saddle up and get ready to rumble! Think of soldiers at war. You don't see them taking extended breaks on the battlefield. I'm sure they're discouraged at times, desiring to be at home with family. But for their assignment, they stay on the battlefield and continue to fight! Let's face it, we all need a break sometime. But for some, this break is entirely too long! Don't take a break when you don't need to.

Sometimes, the breaks are so long that you have to won-der, "Did you take a break or did you give up?" During a church service held the day of my medical school graduation, Pastor Donnie McClurkin spoke a striking statement. He said, "Just because you give up, doesn't mean it's over. Life will still run over you!" I shook my head up and down and said to myself, "Pastor, you got that right!" Even in your stillness, life can run over you! This happens to so many people, but few see its actuality at the time of thinking to give up. Many people give up during a hard task, believing they are escaping that hard task. There are still consequences in giving up! The truth is, not fulfilling your goal not only makes you miserable with regret later in life, but forces you to accept a lesser role or purpose and could also lead you, as it did my shoeless-lady-in-the-rain in California, homeless. Realize that life is hard in itself, so you either work hard to equip yourself to handle life a little better, or you give up and equip yourself with nothing to handle life.

I remember when my mom and I were driving from Co-lumbia, South Carolina, and for some reason, we decided to pull over and take a quick break. It was only an hour-long drive, for goodness sake! Well, our pulling over to stop didn't exempt us from anything, as a lady driving along the highway still hit us from the rear! Here we are thinking we would pull over just for a little bit, as we were tired of driving. You know accidents happen while driving tired. But, even during our break we were still in an accident! You may give up, but know that life does not stop. During this church service, I could only reflect on how I might have turned out if I decided to really quit those times that it crossed my mind. I might have been a prostitute. I might have gotten a job that covers my basic needs each month. Or, I might have hurried and gotten married and lived off the dreams of my husband. So many women have one goal and that is to have a husband. I could have done anything, but I would only have been happy if I had at least accomplished my set goal. So, youth of today, discover a dream, reach for it even through those still moments. And when giving up crosses your mind, fight the thought off and continue to reach forth!

Maybe in the past you've made a move, a mistake. Maybe now you think you've gotten yourself in a difficult place? Between a rock and a hard one at that! Maybe this place is just the wilderness position with a path already laid out for you? So you think you're stuck, huh? Many times we go still because we feel inhibited by our qualifications or others' rules and regulations. We think we are limited, so we dare not venture the impossible. We dare not be the first to do something different and out of the ordinary! We're afraid of the ramifications we think will befall us. You know, like the ones of ridicule for applying for a job others think you're not qualified for, or those of anger from folks because you broke a rule that was *never* supposed to be broken. I remember hearing once, "How could you do that? You know you broke a 'rule' in reaching that goal?" I said to myself, "What rule book are you reading from? I must have missed that memo." I say, as long as it doesn't kill anyone or lead to criminal action against you, don't let anything get in your way. I verbalize that while sort of biting my tongue because some of the great folks of the Civil Rights Movement broke rules leading directly to criminal action, while bringing about much needed positive change.

When you're spirit led, manmade barriers no longer exist! People may hate you for it! While they may think what you've done is extreme and wonder why you "just didn't wait for a better time," you must remember that time waits for no one. If you're not supposed to acquire that particular thing with prayer, God will choose to close that door. Everything we pray for is not necessarily what God wants for us. With prayer, God makes the decision to open or close the door. Anyone who doesn't understand that doesn't understand how God works! How do you know which He will order if you dare not to knock? You knock, but let Him choose! Just because you make a move doesn't mean you must obtain! But with no move, you surely will not obtain anything! You're not a prophet! So stop acting like one by self-prophesying your future. It's uncertain in your eyes, but it is certain in God's eyes.

Divine order demands that God be first in all things. In the state of an emergency, God will break a man-made rule, work a mystical miracle rather than leave His people hurting. I'm a witness to that! If it's not for you, it will not happen. If you upset a few in the process, so be it! For every person you upset, there's another who will be pleased, and there's even another you may be able to inspire. Knock on the door and see if it will open. Run the race and see what will happen. As the old hymnal says, "I believe I'll run on and see what the end is going to be." Go on! But don't go off on a tangent, go off with God!

God made us plain and simple,
but we have made ourselves very complicated.
Ecclesiastes 7:29.KJV

Before I end this chapter, I must communicate on some things that will essentially happen *during* those still moments. Some people go still when they need to move, and others move, when they need to be still. What do you do when absolutely nothing is going on? Are you one of those people who have to stay busy? Do you consume yourself with multiple tasks, inadvertently avoiding being alone? Do those alone times, those still moments actually scare you? Are you a motormouth, constantly talking about yourself, others, or nothing at all, inadvertently avoiding those quiet moments in silence? Do you feel as though you'd lose out on something if you decided to stop, chill out, and be still? Many times during medical school, I felt it was actually being in medical school that was my nothing, and that everything was "on and popping" elsewhere. I felt withdrawn from the world initially, because I was always in the books and in the library! So, you don't have to necessarily do nothing for it to count as stillness. There can be stillness in the routine of things. You can be quite busy and overlook those still moments that exist.

Some of us are actually scared to be still. And rightfully so, as previously mentioned, you can get stuck in those still moments. These quiet, still moments can make you feel empty. It is during these quiet moments alone when the mind wonders. And if you're really down and out, it can be during these quiet moments when you contemplate suicide. If you base your life on others, it can be during those quiet moments when you're unfortunately taught by the world. Ultimately, during quiet, still moments you take a test to live. When they're doing nothing, some people can't help but to be filled with negative thoughts. Suicide is a common one that kills many. When I lived in Columbus, Ohio, it was on a hospital rotation when I realized that suicide is quite common. There were at least two suicide attempts every week at just one hospital during that time! It reached a point where I had to ask myself, "What is really going on and why?"

I remember another beautiful young lady who took a large amount of medication as a suicide attempt in New Jersey. She was the first person in her family to graduate college and was very goal oriented with so much future potential. But she felt abandoned by her family and her boyfriend of many years, who had impregnated someone else. I thought of suicide myself while living in California because I couldn't really see my way. No matter where you are geographically, during those still moments, you're not hallucinating when you hear a voice tell you, "You're not worthy. There's no reason for you to be alive." When it's your time to go, you'll go. You don't *really* want to take your own life. Not knowing what tomorrow brings makes you unworthy to take your own life! Did you hear that? You don't know what tomorrow will bring! Stay alive for tomorrow!

So many thoughts run through your mind in those quiet moments. If you believe that there are two forces in this world, you know that Satan thrives in negativity. Once those tears start to fall, it can be all over for you! Those quiet, still moments are like those 50:50 True or False test questions that I so dislike. It is here when you decide to either go forward or do something else. Something else like suicide, prostitution, drug abuse, or simply quitting a job that really offers you security as it buys you time to find your purpose. You fall into believing that you're just a victim of circumstance. We have to turn those negative thoughts around! We have to attempt to clear our mind and create positive reflecting moments. Learn to get as much as you can out of the small things that occur daily in our lives. There are a few homeless people I see regularly in certain neighborhoods as they, of course, establish their territory. One man, despite his living situation, is always happy and says to me, "I have to be thankful for just another day!"

We all should redistribute the weights in our lives, placing less weight on some big things and more weight on the little things. Let these quiet moments help you appreciate God more; that is, if your mind isn't complicated with thoughts of people and things. God cannot speak to a worried mind. It's not that there isn't room for Him, but rather, there's no room for you to comprehend. If you take some time to be still, you'll realize that the solution to every problem is in God's Word. Stand still when everyone else around you is moving. Sometimes the person standing still gets all the attention. People will ask, "Why are you just standing there?" But, don't let this turn in to, "*Why* are you still just standing there?"

My Granddad used to tell me when I was in high school to, "Go into your closet, close the door, and pray to God." Of course, I never actually went into a closet. I knew he was really saying, "Get away from everyone, get by yourself, pray, and cry your heart out to the Lord." It's OK to be by yourself, without the crowd. It's OK to walk the streets alone. Take these moments and create something positive. You may ask, "What something?" My answer, "Anything something!" In those still quiet moments, as some grow up in the 'hood, it's easy to often look at your surroundings and wonder how could you ever get out of your current situation. When your environment is full of negatives, it's difficult for you to see a better way. You see a successful person on television and think that attaining your goal is such a farfetched idea. Just because you *don't* have doesn't mean you *can't* have!

You do not necessarily have to have a well thought out plan to kill yourself. You don't need pills or weapons. You can be alive, yet dead. Your hopelessness alone will kill you. It kills your spirit and then everything else around you deteriorates. Your health, your home, your will to live…all gone. I remember one lady who just seemed to continue to go down, and fall into severe depression following her divorce. She became obese and didn't do much at all other than sleep and eat. Trying to sleep your way through life only leads to death. I was sad for her children, who had to learn strength from elsewhere, if at all. No one knows the end. You may be hurt now, but you don't know the end! After the darkness comes light! Trust in a better way because depression kills!

So now, you have stood still for some time and you might have all these ideas and creations in your mind that you want to fulfill. I once heard the saying, "Think globally, but act locally." Don't attempt to do too much at one time, but definitely do something! Now, if you've stood still, and still have nothing, you're not steady. Rather, you're lukewarm and it's time to turn the heat up, baby! Stop postponing and procrastinating. Get ready to rumble. Stop escaping reality. You're waiting on a better time, but time isn't waiting for you. Get out of the dungeon and get into the light. It's not always what we say we will do, it is if we actually do what we say. It's not always what we read, it's what we pray. It's not always how we assume power, it's how we live day by day. You are going to do that thing! Stop standing still! Step out!

Chapter Three

THROUGH
THE CHANGE

The Word of God says, "The Lord is not slow in doing what he promised the way some people understand slowness. But instead, God is being patient with you. He does not want anyone to be lost, but he wants all people to *change* their hearts and lives."(KJV) If we look at ourselves, closely that is, we should be able to find something we need to change in order to succeed. Some of us may not even have to look that closely due to the obviousness of the necessary change. When I look back over my life thus far and see how much my progress has been, I can't help but think of what I would have become if I never accepted a change of attitude. Whether your desired change is an attitude change, a job change, a weight change, a change of heart, and/or a change from the past, there are things within us that inhibit us from fully excelling.

I remember being in middle school, seventh grade to be exact, at Davidson Fine Arts School, when I succumbed to fighting a female eighth grader after becoming frustrated with her deliberate and desperate acts of telling lies about me, and attempting to instigate others to be hostile towards me. Having been her friend for a couple of years, she seemed to flip the script

31

and act brand new when the guy she had a crush on began to approach me. She decided to tell others in school to hate me and not be my friend. She even wrote these directions in their yearbooks! People didn't follow her, they didn't disown me, yet what she tried to do made me so mad that one day, after reading her comments in my friends' yearbooks, I just threw my book bag down following class, turned around where she was walking behind me, and slapped her so hard her glasses fell backwards and her mouth fell downwards! I was furious at this chick! We fought for just a few minutes, did the girl-fight thing, shoving each other back and forth, then ultimately received detention for a week. I didn't care about detention because I felt she deserved that slap down! I said to myself and to others, "So what if I have to stay after school for a few days. She got what she was asking for!" I felt relieved, especially after folks approached me with requests to teach them how to fight! I was even more respected now! Needless to say, she never had anything more to say about me again, at least not with my knowledge.

The flipside of this is what happened to me after this brawl. My mom spanked and scolded me so hard, I still can see her expressions of anger. Reflecting now, it's a wonder she never had to see an orthopedic surgeon after that whipping! But her anger didn't stay in my mind for long as even in the next school year, as an eighth grader, I pushed a twelfth grader! I have tried to recall, but I really don't remember what that altercation was about. Maybe it was just a progression from some evil instigated "girl-hating" looks. Probably nothing much at all. But, I do remember receiving three days suspension for a so-called fight that really was only one round of a couple of pushes. This time, I heeded and retained my mom's anger. I accepted the change. And, I also grew up. I remember Rev. Senator James T. Meeks, of Salem Baptist Church of Chicago, said it best when it comes to this fighting and bickering business of high school. I cried laughing at his words, "Why are you worrying about those other kids anyway, causing them to get you all frustrated, bothered, and lose yo' cool. You ain't gone know them four years from now anyway!" And it's true, you really won't know them at all!

Violence is all around us. Whether it is rape, murder, theft, or domestic violence, one thing that everyone, especially a minority growing up in the 'hood must overcome in order to be successful, is the violent nature that surrounds us, or that is within us. How did I grow up and away from engaging in these petty girl-fights and how did this attitude change come about? Well, I realized that there was no benefit to acting like a fool in the streets! There was no benefit in me following negativity so much to the point where I lose myself. Thank God girls were not active in gangs as they are now and that the prevalence of guns was not yet as high as today, or that would've been a serious mess! Suspension from school and detention was certainly not a vacation with my mom! I realized that strong words might have been a better response to these girls. Ignoring them would've been the best response. But I was past the point of words. This is because I had internalized so much of their nonsense that I took myself to a physical point of response.

Now, I know that at least the first girl didn't have anything better to do than to talk about me and write about me in everyone's yearbook! I really should have been flattered, rather than angry. I seemed to be *that* important to her? She was *that* threatened by me that she had to write her last yearly words to others about me! Wow! At first, I didn't see it that way. I didn't see her envy of me. I only saw her attempt to spoil my reputation. So I sought revenge even though the owners of the yearbooks didn't really care what she was writing. Don't wait until you get to a point where you think avenging yourself is the answer. While popular advice spoken around in schools, as I remember it, may be for you to fight at the end of the school year, the safest and best advice is for you not to wait until you get to the point where fighting is the only option. Let it go!

I remember a patient during my first year as a physician who was stabbed in his abdominal area. He survived, but the disheartening thing was that all he could say was how when he got out of the hospital, he "would kill the person who stabbed him." I said to him, "I don't want to see you back in here again." He said, "Oh it won't be me, it'll be him." And I told him, "First, you don't know if you'll get him before he gets you. He might be mad that he didn't succeed in finishing you off! And either way, you'll be dead or in jail! Where is the good?" His response, "Yeah, but I don't know." I thank God that it didn't take me having to go to jail to realize respect for even those who do not respect me. Truth is, fighting was not my true character as I was taught to walk away from "haters." There was one occasion in elementary school when a few girls in my neighborhood disliked me and followed me all the way to my house throwing sticks. Yes, sticks! I never turned back. I did not cry in front of them. I just kept walking home. I had the attitude that my mom taught me, that you cannot do evil and get away with it. Sooner or later it will catch up with you. Girls find the silliest things to dislike each other about. "She dresses nice so I don't like her." Or, "All the guys like her so I don't like her." And let's not forget, "She's not apart of the crowd so I don't like her." Although feeling like a coward then, I now feel peace knowing that I did not fight back. I didn't have to fight back as my mom had the police at the bus stop the next day! Whatever happened to calling the police anyway? Now, people take so much into their own hands, never really solving anything. Seriously, no matter how hard a gangsta is, he/she will still run from the police! In every regard, I felt better resisting the temptation in elementary school than I did throwing the punches in middle school. Now, my spirituality reminds me that we do not fight against flesh, so when you mistreat someone, you're not actually mistreating them, you're mistreating the spirit in them. You don't really know who prays at night. So that should be enough to make you want to love everyone. Today thankfully, all of my schoolmates are alive, all grown up and over the pettiness of childhood. We can all laugh about it. But there are many victims of violence, whether it's of girl-fights or gunshots, that never make it to the point where they can laugh at their trivial fights. Just because you don't value your own life, doesn't give you the right to take someone else's. Just because you hurt someone, contrary to popular belief, life and death is not in your hands! You don't justify yourself just because you are a victim! And just because you don't value your life today, doesn't mean you can't change yourself to recognize the value that *is* certainly in your life. Yes, *your* life!

> And all the trees of the field shall know that I the Lord have brought
> down the high tree, have exalted the low tree,
> have dried up the green tree, and have made the dry tree to flourish:
> I the Lord have spoken and have done it.
> Ezekiel 17:24.KJV

Change, with God, is absolute! And do you see what he can do as in this scripture? Wow, that same tree that is flourishing now, he can change. That dried up, dead-looking tree is one that he can change to flourish. What's high really has no room but to stay level or go down. And what's low has a limitless sky! That alone should be enough to help us be open to go through a change! At some point while doing our dirt, we must accept the change that persecution brings us. During those quiet self-evaluating moments when we hear, "That was wrong," we must yield and grow up. The change may not be automatic. You may change and regress again. But, realizing you were wrong is the first step. For my change, I could not do it alone. I had to seek God, His goodness and His guidance. Know that God doesn't want perfect people, but imperfect people with a heart to be perfect. I had a heart that knew right from wrong and that wanted to be right. And I had a granddad who must have said a hundred times, "In order to live long and be blessed, you must do good to those who do you wrong. That's what I asked Aunt Nini. And she said that's how she was able to live so long."

At another point while doing our dirt, in order to succeed we have to get scared. I know people, especially youngsters, who dance and rump-shake to songs with hip beats, rattling how strong men shouldn't be scared. I love those hip beats and drop-down-low dances, too. The lyrics boost your confidence, although only until the song goes off! We must begin to fear the Lord and value life. Fear is a motivator in itself! Being scared of something can have you go along way! For real! Whether it's the fear of being poor, of being alone, of being in jail, or just the fear of being less than what your destined purpose is to be, don't fear change. Rather, fear what your life will be like *without* the change. Seriously, fear not changing! Learn the difference between good and evil, life and death, and right and wrong. For what seems to be right may in the end lead to a premature death.

There are so many excuses for not wanting to change. One that sticks in my mind is, "I'm destined/supposed to be this way!" Or, "I was born this way. So this is me!" People find various things they are "destined" to be: like being fat, being poor, being an alcoholic, being violent, being promiscuous, and being an underachiever. And everything is blamable on a family history of some sort. For example, "My mom was an alcoholic, so will I be." Or, "My dad wasn't around, so I don't know how to be a father to my child." The truth is destiny is something we choose. Purpose, however, is something that we are placed here on earth to fulfill.

You control your destiny. Lazy people don't want to hear that truth because it means they have to work. Nothing makes me more upset than when I hear someone say they are destined to be fat and/or poor. No way! If that is the case, then there are all kinds of destinies in the world that you could be, and you have to choose the destiny to be fit, healthy and/or successful. Destiny is a choice!

Some people find all sorts of things to change. But it's not their attitude! Although changing your attitude usually is not the first thing to be done, it does fit *somewhere* in the package, you know? Whether it's your nose, your breasts, or your forehead wrinkles, you are willing to pay just about any amount to "nip and tuck" your exteriors, believing this change will automatically result in an attitude change. The fabulous life changing equation has become, Botox + Silicone = Confidence! So we think! I'm pleased that at least my fellow physicians are profiting from this equation, but the patients' "profit" is only a temporary confidence booster. Why not take a look at your inner beliefs first? Have you ever considered the retaliation that may come to *your* family *before* you play into violence? Have you ever considered the thought of another drunk driver calling a taxi so they don't hit your family member, *before you* drive home drunk? Have you ever thought about why it is that you can find something in every other person that they should change, but you can't find anything in yourself?

> Create in me a clean heart, Oh God;
> and renew a right spirit within me.
> Psalm 51:10.KJV

Once you have decided to change, then comes renewal. Isn't it funny how whenever you resolve to make a change, something, someone, or some sinking thought presents itself and interferes with the renewal process? Many times, it's the thought of being "different." Some of us will go along with who we are, although not liking who we are, so we don't stand out by changing. I find it interesting concerning the praise I received from peers after my first physical fight. I'm not exactly sure if people were happy I stood up for myself and fought, or if they were just glad to see a fight. Either way, for a moment their accolades made me feel and think, "Yeah, I'm the bomb!" But I'm glad it was just a temporary feeling as guilt and conviction eventually set in. It's interesting how I didn't receive that many compliments for my excellent violin playing by those same students!

Youth and young adults today live in a culture where it's cool to fight, it's cool to carry a gun, and it's cool for girls to perform oral sex on a guy they clearly know doesn't like them. Although no one had to vocalize it, soon after my second fight, in spite of all the good grades, ballet, instrument playing, leadership roles, and many friends, I became in my mind "the girl that fights." And Davidson Fine Arts would not invite me for another school year. You may try to build a solid character, but one mistake can lead to a formation of a new and damaging reputation. My heart sank as the school principal said to me, "Jerisa, while you are a smart student, we will no longer tolerate your fights." Do you see how even just a couple of pushes can change your course of life and interfere with the renewal? Thankfully, I did not give up, my mom did not give up on me, and I was accepted to an even better school for me. I accepted enrollment at A. R. Johnson Health Science and Engineering Magnet, which was consistent with my attitude renewal.

In this new school community, naturally the "new girl itch" sets in, something has to happen to distract and attempt to get someone off track. At the time, I was wearing colored contact lenses when they first became stylish in the late 80s. They were expensive, but looked good on me. For the record, this is no longer in style! Some girls who knew I didn't have vision impairment were stunned that I had $300 in my eyes. They thought they could get to me by calling me, "Fake eyes!" It didn't work and I wore my eyes until they fell out of style for me. I did not continue in the bad behavior of middle school, following after the negative words and actions of bullies who disliked me for petty reasons anymore. In fact, I specifically made the effort to ignore and turn the other cheek, as my mom again told me I didn't have to prove myself to anyone. She said, "Stand on faith and let God fight your battle, whatever the battle may be. You can be in the world, but not of the world." You see, eventually bullies can come around, respect your confidence, and possibly befriend you, as in my case. Sometimes, it's not a matter of someone disliking you, but rather testing you to see what can be done to get under your skin and control you. Parents, teach your children that they do not have to be a part of the crowd, and that they do not have to subject themselves to violence to be powerful. There is power in silence.

This became evident on an occasion in college when someone I had known and once befriended in my youth, had a change of heart and personality, and in a jealous rage one night at a fraternity party, punched me in the face! Although my friends did think to fight back and were ready to call up an entire posse, I walked away and did not fight back. Even with a bleeding scratch on my nose, I had matured and knew that hitting her back would not have prevented her from doing it, or something worse, again. Had I fought back, I would have been fighting the person, rather than the principle. You can't solve people's psychology with a fist or a gun. When you submit to violence, what you do instead is formulate a cycle of violence. I turned the battle over to God. I forgave her. Unfortunately, she never graduated from Howard. When people come against you with evil, you stand for good. For, as the Word of God tells us, "We wrestle not against people." God didn't give you armor to fight your own battle. Soldiers carry armor. Yet, they meticulously plan the use of weapons for safety and to improve the world's way of life. With guns in their pockets, they not only protect the country they serve, but aid and assist the enemy to build a productive community, a democracy. But, how is it possible for them to *help* the attackers in the midst of war? Here they are in the middle of enemy fire, yet they find ways to support the progress of that same enemy and even *teach* the enemy how to fight! Whoa! Contrary to popular belief, this is not because they are keeping "their friends close and their enemies even closer." They know that if one just fights in a war, there will be no end to fighting! Prayer and God will take you right to the root of the issue—why the person is acting in that manner. Also, he will direct you on if, when, and how, you should respond.

So when this corruptible shall have put on incorruption, and this mortal shall have put on immortality, then shall be brought to pass the saying that is written, Death is swallowed up in victory.
1 Corinthians 15:54.KJV

There are a few people I personally knew that did not accept the change. And it hurts until this day, as I knew their hearts, their potential, and their love for life. But, they got caught up in things of the 'hood. Even though they didn't have to, they

thought of getting lost from them and having to find my way amongst all the trees and unfamiliar pathways was frightening! Driving *by* the wilderness is OK. But, being *in* the wilderness is no joke! Yet, when God knows the path we will take and He's got it all under His control, we don't let Him? Thankfully, He already knows we can be some doubtful people! Isaiah is a very powerful book. Read the above scripture again, and this time, let it saturate your mind. There is an end! Remind yourself that you are free from your past.

> To the hungry soul, *every* bitter thing is sweet.
> Proverbs 27:7.KJV

The change may seem bitter, but eventually it will be sweet. Crying may also seem bitter, but it is part of the renewal. What happens when we cry? So many people think crying is a big no-no! Men are raised with the mindset, "Big men don't cry." However, crying is a form of release. This is evident during funerals when people feel a sense of relief with the grieving process. Crying, a form of weakness, does not mean you are weak, just as much as being alone does not make you lonely! For out of this weakness you can find strength. Have you ever heard of strength being made perfect in weakness? It is what I call purposeful crying. When we cry, we not only become vulnerable, but we take on a form of emptiness. God is attracted to this emptiness, as it opens the way for Him to enter and fill the void. So think of crying not only as a form of grievance, but as a fulfilling way towards rejuvenation. Proverbs Chapter 8 asks us, "Doth not wisdom cry?"(KJV) And Luke Chapter 18 asks us, "Shall not God avenge his own elect, which cry day and night unto him, though he bear long with them?"(KJV)

Have you ever heard someone say, "Honey, I've cried so much I can't cry anymore cuz I'm all cried out!" There is truth to that. But, contrary to popular belief, this isn't because the tear ducts are all dried up, as you can still produce tears. The truth is, the last time you did cry, you became so renewed and so fulfilled that the understanding has stayed firm with you, and because of this renewal you vowed not to return to your former _____ (you fill in the blank). At least you hope to think so! The reality is that there are different types of cries and I'm not recommending for you to cry at every problem, every disappointment. The anointing is not a situational anointing! You cannot cry yourself through every problem! But something does happen when you cry out to God. It is nothing that's tangible and certainly no means to an instant miracle. But it helps to erase your faults, cleanse you, open the door toward God's renewal, and place you back on His path for you!   There were times when I cried out to God and I remember allowing a historic song to be my prayer. I cried, "Lord prepare me to be a living sanctuary, pure and holy, tried and true. And with thanksgiving, I'll be a living sanctuary, Lord, for thee."

It's true that we must get over others' opinions, but sometimes it is ourselves, and our own negative thoughts that we have to overcome in order to change. The yokes we carry are mostly of our own doing. It is our choice! We can be so hard on ourselves and create problems without the assistance of a third party. I've heard many times, "Oh, I want to change, but I just can't do it, at least not now. Maybe later." No one is forcing you not to and no one is keeping you in that bad situation but your own superfluous self-evaluation! I'll never forget one young lady who was so dependent on heroin, that even after experiencing horrible withdrawal symptoms from the drug, she still kept doing it. This lady was laid out on the dirty hospital emergency room floor, crying in pain and vomiting her guts out. Yet, she boldly said to me, "I do heroin everyday. I can't help it." I told her, "If I only had a video tape so you can replay how you look right now, the next time you seek to spend your last dollar to buy the drug, maybe then you'd let go of that habit." Funny enough, the nurse commented, "She pays good money to be in this painful situation. Good money." Clearly, this was not the first time she felt that sort of pain and she knew exactly what harm not changing does to her. But, she chose to avoid the change. She chose to stay locked in that expensive and painful situation.

Likewise, you can't blame others when you are either too lazy, too hopeless, or too satisfied. Get through and over yourself! God can't increase what you don't exercise—FAITH! This faith, tested and proven, needs to be proclaimed! We've been waiting on God to do things, but He's waiting on us! First, realize that you are not perfect. Tell yourself, "The me that I see right now is not the me that I'm going to be." Say it over and over until you get it. Next, allow God to direct you. Develop a relationship with God because you still have power to control your situation. Then, accept the responsibility to take action. Even the angels in heaven, who have already made it, are not just sitting down. Check your burden. If it's heavy it's not God's yoke, it's yours!

Quoting John, Chapter 15, Verse 7, "If ye abide in me, and my words abide in you, ye shall ask what ye will and it shall be done unto you."(KJV) So many people ask what they will in prayer, believing it will happen, yet forgetting the first part of this verse. It's easy to pray for what we want and many people do that. But to let God's words abide in us is more difficult as it means for us to place effort in developing a relationship with Him, which takes time out of our day. It's difficult because it means for us to accept someone else as ruler, rather than we controlling our own lives. Lastly, it's difficult because when we really allow God's words to abide in us, that means giving up those fleshly things we want to do. But, God tells us that we will be able to ask whatever we will, and it will be done! Which means, every benefit you think you're getting from belonging to the gang, every benefit you think you're getting by staying in that abusive relationship, every benefit you think you're getting by being the school bully, and every benefit you think you're getting by being with that already married person can't compare with the infinite and spectacular blessings and peace God has for you, if you would only abide in Him! As my mom says, "People want to be in the light, but they don't want to live right."

I know some people who knew me when I was a child, look at me now and just can't believe I became the first physician in my family, that I was able to overcome so much in the process. They see my single mother, who at times worked two jobs and still had water and electricity cut off at times, and they don't understand how her daughter withstood a dual degree professional program. Heck, I can't myself sometimes! Even my mom, as of 2007, has received her own Doctorate Degree now! Oh, if we rely on Jesus, He will take us to heights we have never even dreamed of. He's ready to do it for you! But, there must be a lifestyle that separates us! No one is perfect. I am not. But, you know what you do that is wrong. If it hinders you, you must let it go.

Somebody said that talk is cheap. I want you to say aloud the following; say it over and over again, believe it and act like you know it. *"Out of my life may Jesus shine. Make me a blessing."* And whenever you begin to doubt yourself, say it again at that time. Because when you decide to do right, when you decide to make a "change for the better," you will be tempted and you will think of returning to your old ways, or the "easier" way of life. If you're not being tempted, that's a real bad thing. It shows that you're no longer in the battle...that Satan isn't worried about you anymore. You're not a threat to his kingdom. It will take constant effort initially as you are; in a sense, retraining your way of thinking about life. Even I haven't fully arrived at this task. It is a daily battle. It will not be easy. But, when it's all said and done, look out for people who just want to keep bringing up your past activities and failures. Do not entertain their sayings, for the popular expression says, "It's not where you've been but rather where you're going." I heard a minister once say that you can beat those people who love you in your past, by telling them first where you've been and what you've overcome, and how you used to be. After that, gladly tell them where you are now and where you are certain to go. It's your choice. Accept the change!

THROUGH
THE TEST

When you attempt the "impossible" task, your desires will inevitably be tested. Your motivation will be tested. And many times during the test to reach the "impossible," you will find yourself questioning the very original ideas and ideals that started you on the quest. When this occurs, the test to succeed can actually lead into another test of your reasoning and ability.

In pursuing education, we take so many tests! Yet, unlike manmade tests, using educational and random guessing techniques will not lead you through to the right answer, when it comes to answering questions about life. You will be unable to look through a test booklet in an attempt to get an idea of how many questions you have left ahead, to answer, and how difficult they may be. You may try hard to figure it out, to rationalize. But, in all your contemplating of this "impossible" task, you will surely fail with your own reasoning. Even without knowing the trials you are destined to face, you *just* have to go through. In taking manmade tests, some people favor the 50:50 ratio given with True or False test questions over the one-fourth ratio of multiple-choice questions. Not me! True or False test questions in my opinion seem so binding and limiting, much like the tests we go through to reach the "impossible" task. In this test, I find the choice is either, [A] to go forward all the way, or [B] to do nothing. It can be a difficult decision, but no one is exempt from the test of tenacity.

When this "impossible" task is finally accomplished and you begin to get congratulations from all those who supported you, and from those who initially doubted you, the path you took can seem to onlookers as a straightforward one. I received a wonderful compliment from a dear friend, also a physician, who knew some of my trials. She mentioned to me how I made it seem so mistakenly easy and that others seeking to follow will surely fail without a co-existing determination. If you happen to be one of these onlookers, admiring the success of others, don't be fooled into following a path, taking a similar test, just because you know someone who succeeded or passed. Maybe there is a different course or test for you to take. Unlike the man-made tests we take in school, which are designated and standard, the test to reach the "impossible" is one that you select. Whether you fail or succeed is also entirely up to you.

And the Lord answered me, and said,
write the vision, and make it plain upon the tables,
that he may run that readeth it. For the vision is yet for an
appointed time, but at the end it shall speak, and not lie:
though it tarry, wait for it; because it will surely come,
it will not tarry.
Habakkuk 2:2,3.KJV

When I started on a journey to become the first physician in my family, I came across this scripture in Habakkuk, which was first presented to me at a Howard University Chapel service by Bishop Donald Hilliard of Cathedral International in Perth Amboy, New Jersey. After graduating college, during my test to achieve the "impossible," I had to revisit this scripture over and over again. It reminded me of how the process, my purpose, although being a difficult journey, has an assured end and I will surely reach the finish mark. It also tells us that we have not because we ask not. I remember once taking this scripture literally and actually writing down my goal one day. Interestingly enough, there is something about actually putting your ideas on paper. It means that you can no longer deny the idea because it is not just a thought anymore. You cannot forget it nor can you erase it.

Whenever you look at it, you will remember the desire. Now, it is permanently plain and all can see or hear! Granted, you can tear it up and throw it away. But to me, it became an unofficial contract and throwing it away would null the contract and thus not reap me any success. I didn't care what got in my way. It would not stop me for two reasons. One, I carry the Lord with me, and two, I was obligated to succeed. I am not one to be easily satisfied! And neither should you be. Why should you be comfortable fixing burgers at a fast food restaurant, when you can be manager of that restaurant? Being upwardly mobile should be the direction we continue to press upon. Why become satisfied being a manager of a restaurant, when you can own that restaurant? Why then be satisfied owning one restaurant when you can own a franchise? Think upwardly mobile! Unless you are certain of your purpose and believe you're serving it now, it's time to take on that "impossible" task, with all of its tests, and ultimately, achieve it.

When you are frustrated because of tests, you can easily pull your hair out until you have nothing left in it but damaged split ends! This is exactly how I felt about the Medical College Admission Test (MCAT). I took this test more than once because I believed that if at first you do not pass the test, retake it. But, even after the last time of my taking it, after I thought I had given it my best, I still hated my scores! I was devastated and thought, "What more can I do?" After all, most medical schools use numbers as a screening tool in their selection process, not offering an interview unless you make a certain percentage. I just didn't think my scores were enough. One of my Program Advisors at the University of California, San Diego School of Medicine, told me he didn't think I was a good enough candidate, as well. Anyone, especially those of lower economic backgrounds, attempting to become "a first in their family" for anything, will undoubtedly face difficulties. When people and Satan say, "That's an awesome task before you and you'll never do that," you must stay firm, knowing that God will protect you. If you don't believe in God, you might wanna consider giving Him a try. But either way, some things are inevitably going to occur that you must go through.

Once I received my scores and after I tuned out the opinions of others, I had to get the nerve to reapply, even with those scores. Ms. Saundra Kirk, of UCSD SOM, helped me to realize that in spite of my average scores, if it was God's will and if I didn't give up, I would reach my goal. So when it seems like your best isn't enough, stand tough. If you've given it your all once, give your all once again. Use what you have without relying on what you have. *You* may fail a test, but God never does. He has the resources. He can open doors that your own intellect can't even imagine to knock on! So, if you don't perform well on man-made tests, you must continue to improve on them. Even though it's hard, if you can get the strength to endure you will inevitably obtain just the right score to have done great on God's test...a test of faith.

God does things to certify that the glory goes to God, not to man!
Proverbs 15:23.KJV

After you've submitted your application, after you've gone on the interviews, and after you've performed in the tryouts, the waiting period that follows is a turbulent time. At least for me it was; I wavered back and forth with thoughts of "not being good enough to obtain" and thoughts of "maybe there's something else for me to do." I must have sent out 25 to 30 medical school applications. After about the first 10 rejection letters started pouring in through the mail, it became automatic for me to assume that each envelope that had a medical school's name on it was just another rejection letter. I cried tears of joy the day I finally received that first thick envelope from my mailbox that said I was selected for an interview. I asked God to forgive me, for I had placed my faith in the wrong places, in my own abilities and inabilities. I had answered the wrong answer to the "faith question." Because truth is, faith does not face facts. God doesn't face facts. I believe God took me through it so I wouldn't think my own intellect did it. Even if I had aced the MCATs, there's no guarantee I'd be the physician or even more so, I would not be the person I am today.

I am not saying to give it *all* to God, as you must prepare to do your part. But, your self-effort can never equal God's effort. Even if you have been rewarded for things gained from your self-effort, the reward is not as lasting as God's reward and does not in any way equate to *His* best for you. Your self-effort has a limitation that you become satisfied with. With God, those same limitations can be exceeded. If you can just develop hope and patience during the test, you'll notice Him make intercessions for you despite your 'have-nots."

Whether your "impossible" goal is in communications, art, a job promotion, athleticism, being a CEO, or a physician, many people have their blessings held up because they are looking at their own qualifications. You should put yourself in a position to receive God's blessing. This takes place when you first realize that you are not "all that and a bag of chips." God not only has all the means but He also has a specific order. I remember attending a night service at St. Stephen's Church of God in Christ in San Diego, that revived me so much at a needed time. Their Pastor, Bishop George D. McKinney, commented during this service, "God is concerned about the seed and what you produce, not necessarily in you, the individual." I remember when I was in my youth when I had a green plant and thought it was so beautiful that it didn't need any help from me. So, I kept it looking pretty in the sun and let it be. Surely, it died within a few weeks and I wondered, "What happened? Why did it die so early?" I started to water it, trying to take care of it and revive it, but it was too late. The damage was already done! Clearly, you don't have to have a "green thumb" to keep a plant alive. You just have to nourish the seed!

During a lifetime, each of us has a seed or many seeds to plant. Planting them well so that they will grow to be plenty and fruitful includes a process of watering and feeding with positive determination, prayer and faith. Even if you live a life filled with destructive behavior, you too, have a seed that will be left long after you are dead and gone. Your seed will then be watered and fed with such negativity that the destruction continues. If you are a parent or grandparent, your children represent seeds of direct offspring. If you allow them to find their own way, catering to nonsense, they will sprout up and be a plant of ugly manner, seeing death in their youth. God is concerned about the seeds you inevitably produce, not in you, the "individual." If you keep this in mind, you will appreciate the ideal that it's not all about you. This belief further positions you in a place to receive God's blessing. So if you don't possess the courage to succeed through the "impossible" test for yourself, maybe thinking of your seed will help you accomplish something.

While we do trust God for the end result, it is possible for us to overlook the process, the blessings that we receive in approaching the finish line. For example, God is not concerned about me being a physician as He is about my patients and my ability to be more than an average physician in the caring of them. He's not concerned about the salary I receive as a physician. He is concerned about the perception of people I come in contact with. There's nothing worse than a cocky, know-it-all doctor who lacks humility. Don't get caught up in the details attempting to figure them out, as you can neglect the blessings that lie within the details. For it is when you're caught up in the details, such as in *your* inabilities and *your* scores, that you can miss the real blessing. Know that the blessing is not just in the final result. It's not only at the finish line. Your blessing also occurs while you're going *through* the test. It is *in* the process of running the race. If you take some time and really reflect on the process to reach the "impossible" task, you'll notice many blessings that occur, which will last much longer after you've retired from the task. In an actual marathon race, for example, the winner breaks through the finish line and receives a reward. That's a huge accomplishment, a blessing! Yet, in the process of preparing for the race, he has strengthened his heart, increased overall oxygenation, improved his immune system functioning, reduced stress, increased energy, and maybe lost a few necessary pounds, all of which are many more lasting blessings than winning the race.

Sometimes passing the test does not only include what you do for you, but what you are willing to sacrifice and do for others in need. When you think you're in bad shape, all down and depressed because you reach a mountain you think you're unable to cross, there is always someone in far worse condition than you, with an even greater mountain to climb. The irony is that God can use someone you think is a heathen or wicked person to help you during the test and demonstrate to you that it's not as bad as it could be. He doesn't always have to use a saint to teach you something. So, if you're looking to find a word of knowledge or wisdom from an "A" student or a high priest only, you just might be looking in the wrong places. God can use anyone to help you through the test.

Late one rare, rainy, chilly night in San Diego, I was leaving a downtown movie theatre after watching *Final Destination*, one of my favorite horror movies. Walking to my car, a lady dressed in rags asked me if I could spare any money. I had no cash on me and had just used my debit card to pay for the movie. I felt really bad. I continued to my car. But she wouldn't leave my thoughts. I was able to collect some change that was scattered about in my car. As I drove around to find her again, I thought I had lost her. In just a few minutes, she had walked quite a distance! Approaching her finally, I noticed she didn't have on any shoes. I immediately thought, "How is she able to walk so fast on these hard, chilly, rain-soaked streets, with no shoes and no jacket?" Her determination was eminent. I became emotional and then the spirit must have led me to take off my tennis shoes and give them to her. They were too big, but of course she found a way to walk in them! I then decided to take a prayer visit to a mountain with a cross, Mount Soledad. This was the first sight that caught my eyes during my initial flight over San Diego. Along the way, I needed to stop for gas. I must have become quite comfortable driving without shoes and had forgotten all about it. So, it wasn't until I stopped at the gas station, with its hard, gritted, and greasy ground that I returned to reality! Uh-oh, I didn't have shoes on! And I'm sure the people at the gas station were wondering what was going on as I could see it in their faces. Remembering what happened leaving the movie, I had stepped outside myself, my problems, and into someone else's problems without thinking about its direct effects on me. It wasn't until I returned to my downtown home and to my closet, after walking barefoot to my apartment complex on the same streets as she that I realized I had given up my only pair of tennis shoes! Moreover, I was not financially able to purchase another pair!

✳ You help yourself by helping others. Yet, there's a distinct difference between giving when you're happily able and sacrificial giving. Whether it is just a sacrificial smile, there's nothing simple about this type of giving when it occurs during a difficult time or test for you. I believed this while living in San Diego. But, it was doubly confirmed when I attended a church service while living in Buffalo, New York, during my junior year of medical school, and at a similar service during my senior year while living in Columbus, Ohio. Both Pastors, of different religious denominations, felt that when you align yourself with a stranger and you pray for that person, something powerful happens. I could fill the spirit flowing heavily in both services as everyone searched for a person they hadn't yet met and prayed for them at that very moment. On these occasions, even in the midst of your hardship, you're more concerned about someone else's nature. When you do this, it's as though you're telling Satan and his negative forces that you're not even worried about your own problems. There's nothing big at all about what you're going through! God has your problems wrapped up. Stepping outside of yourself, your tests of motivation and faith ultimately blesses you. For it lessens your problems, therefore decreasing your worries, and it also shows you that someone else, a stranger, may be worse off than you.

How much do you really want this "impossible" thing? How much are you willing to bear to achieve this thing? How much time, possibly how many friends, are you willing to sacrifice? These are a few test questions that you should consider answering in reaching the "impossible" task. It may seem as though you're giving up a lot. But, ultimately, nothing can compare to the joy of attaining your goal and the happiness that fills you for a lifetime because you've accomplished *the* task! For me, there was nothing traditional about my application to medical school. Some students are fortunate to go straight into medical school with ease, while some other students, because of the competitive nature for entry, take a different route. But, what particularly leads you in reaching the "impossible" task is realizing from the onset that there is definitely more than one way to achieve it!

Getting into medical school, for many, is definitely an uphill battle. The summer before I officially began medical school, there was a brief trial period that some students had to pass in order to progress further. Many of us that summer felt as though there were so many obstacles laid out specifically for us. It was like gambling in a poker game and you just hoped you were dealt a good hand! Ultimately, we were thankful for the opportunity. Yet, not everyone passed the summer full of tests and it was disheartening to see folks work so hard and not succeed. Maybe it wasn't their time or their path. During that summer, I had to believe and constantly remind myself that God would not let me start something that I couldn't finish. He would lead me from the start all the way to the end. That summer, I had to forget about the fact that I was in New York, but my car was stuck in San Diego, impounded two days before my departure and being charged daily fees. I had planned on leaving it at a friend's house in San Diego for the summer, not in the impound yard! Of course, walking outside the day this happened I asked myself, "Why did this have to happen now?" But, I couldn't worry about it. If I did, it would only sidetrack me. So, I packed up my bags and left it without anyone knowing differently. I just had to believe that somehow, in enough time and with someone's assistance, I would get help in retrieving it. The aid happened with my grandmother's assistance, just one day before my car would be auctioned off. Through it all, the entire 29 days, I kept the faith and kept my focus centered on the task at hand, passing the tests. I developed a mindset that there's no stopping me. And so I've learned to believe in the saying, "When things go wrong, I count it best."

God is not a God of circumstance. He doesn't work according to what things appear to be. He doesn't follow science and wonder. They follow Him. So you've tried to accomplish the "impossible" task and failed. Now it is as though you're standing at a mountain weeping because you can't figure out how to cross over. It's also possible that you're alone without comfort because no one wants to be with a downhearted person at the bottom of a mountain! When you are at this point, you cannot rely on anyone. Help may not come pouring to meet you at the bottom of the mountain. So, save your disappointment by not looking for it! Even if you have many words of encouragement from a few, all these words mean nothing if you can't decide to go on and make the way. So what if the mountain's high? So what if you failed the first time? There's no better way to fail than to allow your ego to justify you. Get rid of the ego and consider why you failed.

Some people fail because the idea (or test) was too premature. It wasn't really your time or maybe your real purpose. Perhaps you started the test for the wrong reasons, making you take the wrong test. Some people fail because they *need* to retake it, to redo it. However, are you less of a person because you failed? No way! Actually, you're more of a person. With every time you retake the test, you learn more, gain something. If it's the first time failing the team tryouts, you either strengthened your muscles to excel the next time, or you learned who loves you for you and not for your success. If it's failing losing weight, you either learned your limits to exceed next time, or you learned who your support system is and is not. If it's failing the small business venture, you either learned mistakes not to remake, or you learned who your investors are and are not. Even at the mountain that seems so fierce, even when your disappointment is testing your strength, God can place you on the mountaintop with your next attempt. He can give you answers to very important questions. So go ahead. Retake the test!

While you may not see the mountain coming, you must be ready. How do you ready yourself? I must say I was not always ready. But soon, scriptures flowed through me and I remembered who was in charge, who had gotten me this far. I also remembered that there was another force at work to destroy me that didn't want me to succeed. I knew that I wanted Jesus to ultimately be in control and I was determined not to let Satan win over my life. You can never be fully ready for something, it just happens. But, you can be ready with a positive outlook, which governs your response.

Whether we succeed or fail, when we come near the end of a test, there is definitely a sweet smell of relief! We're elated that it's almost over! But unlike man-made tests, where the last few questions are generally not trick questions, you can be shocked by events that could occur approaching the achievement of your "impossible" task. During my last academic semester in medical school, I was just leaving Hofstra University after studying late one night when I remembered something I needed to tell my friend. I turned around and quickly ran to give him a message, but he was gone. Well, my book bag was so heavy and I was already carrying more books in my arm. So, I left my bag in the walkway, as it would only take a minute. When I returned to my bag, a security guard was waiting nearby. I picked up my belongings and proceeded to walk when he approached me and said, "I'm gonna have to search your bag!" Of course my response was, "You have to do what? Why?" I was totally shocked. I said, "Dude, it's late and my brain is saturated. You've got to be kidding me, right?" There I was, trying to tell him that I study there all the time and I'm not a criminal! No one I knew was around to vouch for me at the time. I thought it was a joke, but he wanted to let me know he was serious. I had nothing more to say to him except "Whatever dude," and followed his power-tripping commands. I was tired, irritable, and disgusted, as I was just trying to get my study on! Next, I'm being escorted over to the office, had my photograph taken and was banned from the college!

I remember asking this Black female security guard what the commotion was all about and why he took the bag so serious. Apparently, the security guards were on tight response. It was post 9/11/01 and something was going on in Manhattan and New York, which caused them to be on Red Alert. He suspected I had a bomb or something. Really. And my frustrated demeanor didn't help the situation either. So, I could no longer study at my favorite area library. Talk about being tested at the end while studying for the last test! Thankfully, school session was almost over and most of my studying was too. If you've ever taken a test in harsh environments, you know exactly what I mean. Whether it's battling to take a test in a hot classroom when the AC is broken or there's loud noise outside, eventually you learn to deal with the roughness of a situation. Likewise, in the test of life to reach your "impossible" task, there are moments you must resist panicking when things go out of the norm. Don't stress out and hold your breath approaching the end, but proceed with caution! Anything could happen!

Even at the end, you may find yourself in slight distress. "Blood, sweat, and tears" is a great cliché to describe medical school. Tears that appear toward the end are mixed with thoughts of frustration and thoughts of joy knowing the end is already nearing. While I was preparing for three of my final MBA exams in Bethlehem, Pennsylvania, I cried hard. Really hard. But it was in frustration. Overwhelmed, I even gave up momentarily. I cried because I thought I couldn't do it. It just seemed to be too much to juggle at one time! Yet, if I stayed in that temperament, I would not have finished. Sometimes you can cry so much that instead of becoming fulfilled and renewed, you become weak and hopeless. Those tears were leading me down a hopeless route! I had to wipe my eyes, study on through my fatigue and realize that even if I failed, I did not quit in the middle. Moving closer to the end, you can get tired. But just like the energy pulled by a marathon runner as he nears the finish line, you must draw from deep within yourself the determination needed to press on. Wipe the tears! It's almost over!

There should be no talking during the test! Remember when the teacher used to remind the class of this? I know a few people who took licensing tests more than once, and each time they failed they felt so guilty in having to tell their folks of the failures. One of them was so excited about taking the test, even though she wasn't prepared, that it seemed she told the entire city! I know it helps to have support, but do you have to tell everyone? You bring the embarrassment of failing to yourself because you can't keep from telling everyone your plans! I've been there, having to show face after "missing a beat" and it is not too comforting. The burden of failing is compounded with the embarrassment of having to tell people of the failure, some of which offer no encouragement after hearing you failed. When the young lady was sad because she had to tell so many people of her failure, I could only think, "Why did you have to tell the whole community anyway?" Likewise, you think you've met your husband or wife? Does this mean you have to tell everyone in church before you even get the marriage proposal? If you do, in a year you may have to also tell them how you've found a new husband and that you were confused. Stop talking to everyone during the test and let the process be.

Some people turn various obstacles around from God testing them, to them testing God. Be careful not to turn the test into one that God has to take. When you pray for something, God gives you the answers. Maybe you don't realize it, or maybe you realize it, but deny it. Ultimately, when you deny it, you're questioning his answer. Now, you're testing Him! Automatic failure!

My mom used to tell me that God does not work in the natural realm and thus, some people will never understand His works. God can and will take you through the test. But in the process, you may ask, "Why am I going through this?" Particularly, I believe God does things to show you to stop depending on your abilities and on people. He gives us the desires of our hearts. However, He desires to get the glory, not man. So, while you take the test to reach the "impossible" task, don't quit, don't cave in, don't be discouraged and depressed. God said it! He will do it! When He does something, don't second-guess Him! Believe it and it's settled! Now that you've withstood the test, now that you've hung on, now that you've arrived, don't be satisfied. Ask God for something else. He'll even give you more than you ask. Yes, you will take even more tests. But, unlike manmade tests, you are now equipped with the answer key!

Chapter Five

THROUGH
THE HEALING

Diagnosis is a powerful word. Yet, even being a physician, a diagnosis in itself means little to me. A diagnosis, defined by Webster's New World Dictionary is "the act of deciding the nature of a disease, situation, problem by examination and analysis," and/or "the resulting decision." I could never imagine that in my own quest to become the first healer in my family, I would need to be healed. Therefore, I've learned that the real meaning of diagnosis is not the diagnosis itself, but rather what *you* mean to do now that you *know* the diagnosis.

Before we are ever diagnosed with anything, we should know that character is built out of circumstance—every circumstance. If Satan couldn't use anything else to detour me, battling me with my health would prove to be a real fight. I didn't realize how many times I had received a diagnosis myself until after two years I received a call reminding me of a bill that needed to be paid. Here I am thinking at the time that they were all paid! Yet, I remembered there had been a time when my mom and I were confused as to which medical bills where paid after we passed a couple over to my dad for assistance. The bill collector informed me that I had been to the hospital five times in a span of two years and that there was still one left. I was absolutely puzzled and insisted she read the dates and the diagnosis to me as there was no way I had been ill that many times during medical school! She couldn't tell me each diagnosis, so I was left only to reflect. But, I knew that with my interest in Emergency Medicine, there was absolutely no way I would allow myself to sit in the hospital for three plus hours waiting to be seen for a diagnosis that was not severely painful or serious!

> Beloved think it not strange concerning the fiery trial which is to try you, as though some strange thing happened to you. But rejoice, in as much as ye are partakers of Christ's sufferings, that, when his glory shall be revealed, ye may be glad also with exceeding joy.
> 1 Peter 4:12,13.KJV

The saying, "Times are filled with swift transition," is so true. In just a 24-hour period, a life change can definitely be made. An old, historic gospel song sheds light on this as well, with its lyrics, "Build your hopes on things eternal. Hold to God's unchanging hand. Life is filled with swift transitions, none on earth will be unmoved." Many times, these swift transitions are due to health issues, car accidents, and injuries. How do we get through it when we are so weak not just from the illness itself, but also from the prognosis? And why does God allow these diagnoses to happen? Well, there is nothing good or bad that happens on earth. For what Satan means for bad, God means for good. One of the first symptoms that bring patients to doctors causing them to hear of a diagnosis, is pain. Yet, there's nothing funnier than when I speak to patients who actually fear taking pain medications for their chronic conditions because they have "heard of the side effects." I look at them with amazement while they struggle in their pain, simultaneously requesting some other alternative, only to hear me tell them, "You need to take your meds and stop wallowing in all that pain!" It's not initially the actual diagnosis patients must get through, but pain.

Late one Wednesday, one of my best friends and I were at Hofstra University's 24-hour study hall. My pain started somewhere between 9:00p.m. and 11:00p.m. And as time passed, the pain intensified. I mentioned it to her, but the pain was initially so vague, all I could describe was, "My butt hurts." There was no way for me to stop studying because I had an exam that following

Friday. So I took a few breaks, walked around and sat down to study again. Soon, while reading up on cardiology, the pain became so unbearable that I was forced to start crying, "What is this?" But, I kept studying through the tears with my friend who regularly asked me if I was okay. I ignored the pain for as long as I could. We had planned to study all night. Then, I gave in, looked up and told her I was going to the emergency room! It was now between 3:00a.m. and 4:00a.m. She offered to go with me. I refused the offer, as I didn't want to interrupt her study schedule. But, I must have cried all the way, while driving to the ER.

The familiar statement is so true, "Doctors are the worse kind of patients!" Unfortunately, I couldn't give the emergency room doctor much of a history, but my rectal exam revealed blood. So she, not giving me any answers, referred me to a specialist. In school, we had not gotten to gastroenterology yet. But, upon waking the next day after lying in bed all night, I realized the pain had dissipated. It was a positional pain, so I thought, "Could this be what I think it is?" I called the doctor's office to arrange an appointment and followed through with the bowel prep, not an easy thing to do. And the flexsigmoidoscopy, which I was a little scared to go through with, verified my sentiments. All I could think during the exam was, "This doctor had better make this quick!" The diagnosis...hemorrhoids! Thankfully, the gastroenterologist said I did not need surgery.

Like every other human who gets this state of being, I asked, "How did this happen? How long will I have to deal with this?" Every time I sat down, the pain occurred. Then, I had to *really* ask myself, "How am I going to sit down to study...to sit down at lectures?" I was unable to find any good conclusion to this diagnosis. My mom showed me no sympathy. She said forcefully to me through the phone, "Why are you just sitting there wallowing in your pain?" I replied, "Why shouldn't I?!" She said angrily, "So are you going to sit there and waste energy? You need to get a backbone, girl!" She was not consoling at all. But, she was right! I needed to get mad, not sad, about this ailment. I began to pray for revelation and strength from God. And I received it after reading the book of Ephesians. I did not adapt to those hemorrhoids, they had to adapt to me! I was not going to allow this thorn of diagnosis to rule me! I realized I couldn't do anything without God. And if it doesn't kill me, it makes me powerful. I decided to start studying at home, lying down. My answer to Satan was, "I don't *have* to sit down to study!" By this time, I was determined to find a way through this. Fortunately, my school was beginning to implement the daily recording and downloading of lectures for review outside the classroom. This was perfect for me! I didn't *have* to sit in classroom all day to hear the professor. For the length of time I would be able to stay seated, I could schedule to go to the computer room. My friend who knew the situation would call and check on me. Eventually, we would laugh at my response, which was jokingly, "I'm just laying down studying, girl. Just laying down." And she would say, "Work it out, girl. Do the dang on thang!"

I found a way to fight even without understanding the situation. Then, I began to thank God for the hemorrhoids and for the course at school he had arranged for me to be able to study, in spite of the diagnosis. Soon, I had faith that I was never going to need surgery for the hemorrhoids and I was not going to have to fight them all my life. I'm glad to say that the whole ordeal lasted less than five months. As a physician, I'm reminded of this situation when patients require surgery and I'm so thankful that I survived that diagnosis and didn't let it interfere with my goals. And even now with all of my sitting down, I haven't had pain since then…June of 2002. After the tears, after the denial, and after the doubt, you must find a way to fight on through the pain.

So, Paul said, "Much rather will I gladly glory in my infirmities.
Therefore, I take pleasure in infirmities, in reproaches, in necessities,
in persecutions, in distresses for Christ's sake.
2 Corinthians 12:9-10.KJV

A Howard University's Chapel speaker once said, "Tough times don't last, tough people do! You have to learn how to take it. Then, you'll learn how to shake it. Then, you'll make it." We have to accept what God allows, be thankful in the small things, and everything else will be added. In your quest to be successful, you may be well on your way in a stable place using your same adequate approach that you have become accustomed to. But when something like a diagnosis occurs to interrupt your flow, your unique methodology, accept it and do not allow it to shake you. With patience, you'll discover new ways to continue toward success, regardless of the diagnosis. It only rules you when you allow it to do so. So many times we get a diagnosis and we worry, become anxious, and apprehensive. Worrying is such a negative meditation! It begets nothing but more worry. You can never worry yourself to the point of peace! It just doesn't happen that way.

You can however, worry to the point where you are hopeless, afraid to take action, and have created another diagnosis for yourself, like a stress-induced stomach ulcer. You cannot lean unto your own understanding, as Proverbs tells us. You must instead, take pleasure in the infirmities and necessities. I'm sure you ask, "How, Jeris, did you take pleasure in *that* pain?" Yes, it was a miserable pain. I learned how to "take it"! I realized I could not fight, and actually was not even fighting against, the actual diagnosis. But rather, I was fighting against the principle. You're not fighting Diabetes; you're fighting the principle of Diabetes. You are not fighting strokes; you're fighting against the principle of a stroke. Satan uses these things to steal, kill and destroy not our bodies, but our spirit, then our soul! So fighting principles becomes a fight of the spirit. In order to fight the spirit, you *have* to change your mind. Even if you have an incurable disease, there is still a healing of your soul.

There was a specific thought I developed during that particular illness. I believed that you come to a place in your spiritual experience where your will, will be God's will. And His will, will be your will. There is a difference in praying for God's will in doubt, and for God's will in hope. We are made in his image. He created us to be like Him. So, there is a point where we should be able to command that His will be our will, too. In my opinion, this is how we learn how to "shake it"! It was this thought that enabled me to demand to my diagnosis that I be healed! Forsaking all the pain and the distraction it caused to my studies, I took God on His Word. You see, God can do no mighty works with an unbelieving spirit. No matter how much you say you'll be healed, if you don't really believe what you're saying, you're wasting your voice, honey! When you're doubtful of yourself and Him, why should He heal and deliver you? I developed a backbone and then found ways to cope and get through that diagnosis. And there was never a more opportune and convenient time for my school to download lectures for computer access! Talk about making ways! God prepares a line of attack through your problem. Not only that, but there's something He wants you, yes you, to gain from having the diagnosis. You'll only discover this once you've rid yourself of that unbelieving spirit. Shake it off! Your prayer is still unanswered because your faith is not active.

> Be careful for nothing, but in every thing by prayer and supplication,
> with Thanksgiving, let your requests be made known unto God.
> And the peace of God, which passeth all understanding, shall keep
> your hearts and minds through Christ Jesus.
> Philippians 4:6,7.KJV

Are you looking *up* or are you looking *at* your misery? Or, are you just *ignoring* your misery? Either way, God can bring misery into light! God will permit the destruction. It's interesting how unbelievers ask, "If God is so good, why did He create cancer?" I'm thinking, "Duh?" Don't they know this is the same God that destroyed the ancient civilizations? What do they mean how can He create cancer? He's God. This is His world and He does what He wants. That's the whole point! However, the destruction is not necessarily for your ruin, but for your restoration. As a child, there were times when I'd see neighbors burning their yards and think, "Why on earth are they setting fire to their yard? They're burning the grass and everything all up!" My mom would tell me what I'd also read later, that when you burn, although it seems harsh, you're creating a better, rich soil. Ultimately, you're making it better for the new green grass to come through. After the destruction, comes a rebirth.

In October 2003, when I found a lump in my right breast, I disregarded it. I know, I know, "How could I ignore a lump?" There is not a good excuse as the action is definitely something not to repeat. For me, it occurred during the middle of the hardest school year and there was no way I would let this be another distraction. It was, however, scary to let go. I thought it was a bad time. For, I had exams to pass! Nevertheless, you cannot ignore your diagnosis for very long, as you will be forced to face it in time. Just hope the time you waste disregarding it does not hurt the situation even more, as it does in many cases. For me, waiting proved to be no help at all, as there was never a *better* time to deal with the diagnosis. It had been five or six months since my discovery when I finally conferred with a doctor. She felt it was either a cyst or a fibroadenoma, both common in many women of childbearing age. She simply stated to watch it, recommending no tests. But by this time, I was concerned and desired to have whatever tests that needed to be done in order to be exact on its description. So, I insisted she refer me to a Radiology Center, where I was initially told that a Fine Needle Aspiration (FNA) would be performed. I refused a friend's offer to come along, as I felt comfortable with the FNA because the procedure is really quite simple. For that reason, I arrived alone. But, when I arrived and was lying on the table after the ultrasound, I was told that I would instead need a core biopsy, a more intense procedure. Instead of a fine needle, it would be a machine-like gun that sounded like an old stapler machine, clicking through my breast tissue. The doctor's description alone made my eyes buckle as though I was saying, "You've got to be kidding me, right?" My breasts had become quite voluminous and I was apprehensive of possible scarring. Almost reluctantly, I agreed to have it done that same day. I thought enough time had passed already. I endured, and the result my doctor first told me was a simple fibroadenoma. Thankfully, there wasn't really a scar at all. I was relieved and could again entirely focus on my coursework.

To my surprise, it wasn't over! Three weeks later, one day before my leaving New York for summer break and moving out of my apartment for hospital rotations, my doctor called and left a detailed message on my voicemail that the initial results were not complete and I indeed had more to be concerned about. She then read a diagnosis, on my voicemail, of an atypical hyperplastic (more than benign) fibroadenoma, with many additional diagnostic words. She mentioned the name and number of a breast surgeon, as well. I would require breast surgery! Hearing all this on my voicemail, with no immediate way to have my questions answered, was one insensitive thing, but the timing couldn't have been more inappropriate. I mean, I was only moving out of my apartment in Long Island, New York, to go to Augusta, Georgia, and finish studying for the first step of the medical board exams I was to take in less than four weeks! Before attempting to even call this doctor back, I remember being outside, sitting on the ground in the middle of campus at a pay phone, crying a river! I called my mom and granddad trying to figure out what I would do. I remember thinking, "Here I am, moving out of my apartment, studying for an important exam, and here she is now telling me I need surgery and to see a breast surgeon ASAP! My dad and aunt are already on Interstate 95 North coming to help me move out today! What am I going to do? And how am I going to pass this exam? I can't even focus anymore!" It was shocking to everyone involved. But through their own worry, my mom and granddad attempted to comfort me over the phone. They must have said all sorts of things during that telephone conversation. I heard their voices. Yet, I was unable to organize and regard much of what they were saying. My mind had never been so blank! I didn't want to do anything! I didn't want surgery and I didn't want to finish studying!

If we are faithless, God still remains faithful for he can't disown himself.
2 Timothy 2:13.KJV

The next day, I went to see the recommended breast surgeon, along with my dad and aunt. As he described the surgery to me in a way that was sort of horror like, I perceived his bedside manner to be much less than adequate. In my opinion, he had little consideration for a woman's breast. Maybe it was because he knew I was in the medical field? But regardless, I was not impressed with what he had to say, nor how he said it. So, I would defer the surgery until I was again in New York and I had found a surgeon whom I could trust. My dad and aunt helped me pack and move out of my apartment as we originally planned. Back in Augusta, I was able to regain my composure and concentration to study for the upcoming exam. I didn't have a surgeon. My duration for being in New York under good health insurance was short and periodic, and I was moving all around for hospital rotations. Despite this, and although I didn't yet know where I would stay during the time of surgery, I would not allow myself to be in constant dismay. This time, although ready to get the surgery over with, I was forced to wait until God's appropriate time and order was in place. Until then, I could not be consumed by it. I had to continue to work toward success. I turned the diagnosis over to God. Even though I didn't understand what was going on and why God chose that time to teach me something, I would not throw my hands up and quit. No matter what, I would not faint and I would fight on!

This diagnosis, with all the changes and stress that came along with it, was a big detour, a setback. It was disappointing.

But disappointments don't change our appointment set by God. The spirit of Man is like a burning candle. The flame, although heating the candle making it very hot and bothered, never actually touches the candle. The wick burns *through,* heats and shapes the candle. After being shaped, the candle wax is all gone, but the spirit of the smell can still be appreciated with a sniff of the glass. So is our spirit still appreciated after death. We are to be shaped during our lifetime. So when you get into hot trouble, know that you too, are being shaped. Although a heated time for me, I was being shaped. I realized that God was going to use me, to shape me to go out and heal, that he was taking me to greater places. He was ultimately trying to produce something in me. Pastor Donnie McClurkin gave a timely message at Perfecting Faith Church in Long Island, New York, where he stated, "Trials make us more than average." Think about it—who likes or even wants to be average? No one! If we all became a people who saw our problems as making us more than average, nothing would get us down! Likewise, I believed this diagnosis would make me more than an average physician. I believed I would be able to relate to my patients. And I believed as the Scripture tells me, "The righteous have never been forsaken." I stood firm and kept a positive attitude. I was reappointed with God. I passed all steps of both the COMLEX and USMLE Medical Boards, the first time taking each.

Jeanne Guyon's *Experiencing the Depths of Jesus Christ* explains, "God is just looking about for people who will remain faithful and loving even when He has withdrawn himself." It was a trying time finding a surgeon, finding a time when I would be in New York, and finding a place to stay. But through all the searching, God can work things out at the *last* moment—at His moment. Even when the problem seems too big for you, it's just right for God. He's still working and He does so until perfection! There was no way I could have planned the date, doctor, and living arrangements better than He. Really! It had been almost a year since receiving the diagnosis. Finally, the surgery occurred and did so smoothly.

Surgery of any kind can be scary. For me, it was weird getting through the idea of sedation. You are essentially giving your life over to someone and you hope while you're tranquilized they do as they said to you, while you were awake. In the operating room, before the anesthesia set in, I witnessed being strapped to the bed. A horrible feeling! I really think the O.R. team should wait until the patient is fully sedated before they go strapping folks down, as it does feel a bit creepy, adding to the anxiety. After the restraining, I prayed for God to rule in the surgeon as never before. And before I was fully sedated, I was able to insist to the surgeon that he place the incision at a location juxtaposed to my areola (nipple) for scar reduction, as I saw him drawing on my skin to cut through a different area than what we discussed during our previous consultation. Even with all the surgeries I've been a part of as a medical student, I made sure to remind the team to wake me up after it was all over! Soon, it was finished. When I awoke in the recovery room, there was a peace that settled upon me.

Nay, in all these things we are more than conquerors through Him that loved us. For I am fully persuaded that neither death, nor life, nor angels, nor principalities, nor powers, nor things present, nor things to come, nor height, nor depth, nor any creature, shall be able to separate us from the love of God, which is in Christ Jesus our Lord.
Romans 8: 37-39.KJV

Cancer! We all hate it! Although my surgical results ultimately proved to be benign, there was always a possibility of a hyperplastic (premalignant) course progressing to an atypical (malignant) course. So the idea never escaped me. One thing I realized from my and others' diagnoses, including my beloved grandfather's, is we do not die *from* a diagnosis. We die *with* it. And if we die *with* a diagnosis, we should die fighting it. No other example can I attest to except with what a particular group of individuals did on a plane that landed in Pennsylvania on September 11, 2001. They knew they were about to die, but they did not sit down, they did not only die crying. Many of them called out to God, landed, and died fighting. Psalm 68: 20 tells us, "He that is our God is the God of salvation; and unto God the Lord belong the issues from death." Through God, we can escape death and beat it. So, even if your body is never healed, your spirit can be and Satan therefore, has no victory because you did not give in just because you felt God placing you at your end. If we can think of cancer or other bad diseases as coming along *with us* for the ride, rather than killing us and causing us to die *from it*, we take control, even in our weakness.

When things look as though they are not in your favor, don't give up. This is the time to talk to God. You don't have to wait until you're at your end before you ask God the questions, "Why, When, How, and Can you, Lord?" The year 2004, the beginning of my last year in medical and business school, proved to be one of the most difficult. Having to move around for hospital rotations was one thing, but when my grandfather became ill, my spirit was tormented. First, the family became aware of a prostate nodule that apparently my grandfather had known existed for some time. I decided to take a few vacation days off from a rotation to be present at his biopsy. At that time, the urologist told me in an empathic manner that there was no doubt in his mind the nodule was large, asymmetric, cancerous, and not in a location for surgery. He mentioned to ultimately wait for the conclusiveness of the biopsy test, but with his experience, his opinion scared me. I thought if the doctor didn't know, he would simply say he doesn't know. At least, that's what I do. So, I believed as he did, that my grandfather had prostate cancer and that the biopsy would verify exactly what he had stated. I was faithless, as I had already heard the diagnosis from the doctor. But, my mom said she would not believe it yet.

After a rough waiting period, I was shocked with excitement as my mom and grandfather called me revealing a benign result from the biopsy. I asked them in disbelief, "Are you serious?" Boy, was I guilty, not in believing the doctor's preliminary diagnosis, but in not waiting on and believing in God. I asked for forgiveness and learned a few valuable lessons. Your faith should not stop when things look bad or when the doctor simply says it's bad. And never, as a physician, give a preliminary conclusion based on experience with how things look before the results come in, as there is never a firm or universal equation.

My grandfather was just two weeks into his way to recovery from prostate surgery when he developed blurry vision. These changes worsened very rapidly. Initially, his ophthalmologist recommended surgical removal of his cataracts and had scheduled a date. But, on the day before the eagerly awaited surgery, my grandfather was referred to another ophthalmologist who disallowed the surgery because of her findings of a blood clot. My grandfather, who was so prepared for cataract surgery, was devastated! This doctor not only mentioned a delay of up to a year for the surgery, but also told him there was a 50:50 chance of him going completely blind even with her recommended laser surgery. I had no idea his eyesight was that bad! He could hardly see to eat! I received this news as I drove from my residence in Allentown, Pennsylvania, to Olympia Fields, Illinois, just outside Chicago, for a residency interview. With this diagnosis, I would not believe in a physician's ratio, but in healing. Yet, I had never heard my grandfather so spiritually weak! He had received so many diagnoses lately. He cried. He wanted to give up. In his mind, it was over. Through my tears, I insisted he give the laser treatments at least one month. In faith, I guaranteed some improvement. When I hung up the phone, the thought crossed my mind, "Is that really possible, Jeris?" But I wouldn't give up. Within three weeks, his eyes were starting to clear and were responding to the treatments. That was indeed a Halleluiah time! Of course, the physician was amazed with his progress. Soon, things were finally starting to calm down. His Foley catheter was finally removed from the prostate surgery and he was now starting to read the newspaper again! But this relief would only last a couple of weeks.

I was just starting a new rotation in Newark, New Jersey, when I received a phone call from my mom stating that my grandfather was found in a confused state wandering on a major highway with no shoes or shirt. My only response was, "Huh? Run that by me again! I don't think I heard you correctly. Are you talking about *my* granddaddy?" Although we had noticed some change in his short-term memory in the month prior, we were not ready for whatever this was. Thankfully, I still had vacation time left to take off, time that would have to be made up at the end of the year. So, I drove all night to Augusta, Georgia. I never knew I could stay awake 40 hours straight! I did not stop until I got to his hospital room on Christmas Eve where I found him strapped up and restrained in every way possible. I was in a rage with what I saw! The thought of him not attending or even remembering my upcoming graduation hooding was hard, because his wisdom and encouragement were the reasons I made it through the many times I thought of giving up. We received an extensive differential diagnosis list. It was a shock to everyone! On Christmas Day 2004, my grandfather was still hospitalized and still in a confused state. I did not know whether his health would go up or down, but

I did know that God was in control. Believing that and saying it repeatedly was the only thing that got me through each day.

How do you endure when your health seems to continually go poor at the "wrong" time? How do you keep your determination to be healed when, as soon as you taste relief, another problem presents itself? My answer is to hold on to God's Word and even in your weakness, see His love. My grandfather's delirious state did not last too long. Though it took months of healing from everything he had experienced, we were glad the day my grandfather drove again and when he was well enough to remember my medical and business school graduation. Think of every bad turn in your quest to be healed, as a resting place in route to a final destination. When that mountain rock comes to take you off track, take a seat, catch your breath for a moment, and then move on. But, the only way it becomes a true resting place, not a stressful one, is if you stay firm in your belief of who is in control. Learn to be thankful in the "small" things and the "little" signs of healing that God gives you. As the Word tells us, He will never give you more than you can bear!

Often people suffer from gallstones, kidney stones or stones located in the ureters that exit the kidneys, all being very, very painful diagnoses. I was prone to experiencing painful, periodic and recurrent salivary gland and duct stones that inhibited me from eating during my junior and senior years of medical school. I would be so hungry after working in and running around hospitals, but if I even attempted to eat, the gland would enlarge and hurt severely! The first time this happened, I cried in frustration, not really realizing what was going on. I was even told by one ER doctor that it was lymphadenopathy (swollen lymph glands). Boy, was he so wrong! The second time this occurred, I was mad with disgust, having to see a specialist for stone removal. The third time this transpired, I had no negative response at all!

During this time, in addition to my medical school rotation, I was preparing for my last three and most difficult exams to complete my Masters in Business Administration. Instead, with this occurrence, I laughed with my friends and even willingly revealed it to interested students during that rotation. After all, we were all learning medicine! There I was in pain, barely eating and showing my mouth around to other students as though I was proud! I could just imagine Satan saying in shock, "She's actually happy about that salivary stone and showing it off this time!" I developed my own technique for removing the stone, which was using heating pads and drinking plenty of water. By that time, I had adapted and would not let this diagnosis upset me or alter my state of being. I was absolutely tired of that! Now, I was trained to succeed through this diagnosis and could no longer be swayed or distracted by it. The time of my showing it off was the last time this stone occurred!

There are at least three thoughts to learn from this diagnosis. The first is that I gladly took control of my health. Sometimes we need a doctor and sometimes we need self-motivation. It was self-motivation that helped me conquer the stone that final time and find ways to remove it myself. You should take action in your own treatments. If you know you're a diabetic, why continue to pig out and eat so many sweets? If you know you have cancer, why deprive yourself of powerful anti-oxidants by not eating fruits and vegetables, along with taking chemotherapy? The second thought to learn is the attitude I developed. I gladly demonstrated the diagnosis to others. Oh, how Satan must have really been mad! Here he was trying to get me down in my spirits with this diagnosis because of the pain and starvation it caused, and here I was showing it off like it was a gift! The questions I asked myself were, "How can I continue to cry up a river at something that kept on making me stronger? How can I be mad at something that only seeks to bring me closer to God?" Get glad! The last thought is how I did not let this diagnosis stop me. I didn't take any sick days off! At work, when I told the doctor and resident I was working with what I had, they looked somewhat in disbelief. Here I was in pain and, with the love of food that I have, not being able to eat. Yet, I was pleasant and smiling, as though I had no stone! Some people try to ignore the pain. But, when you try to ignore the pain, you are really taking no action to overcome it. Ultimately, it consumes you in your ignorance. Instead, don't just sit back and ignore the pain, still letting it get you off track. Instead, accept it, swallow it up, and fight through it.

Lastly, we have to stop relying on the diagnosis and treatment to get us through life. Psychiatric conditions are perfect examples. We have become a society so reliant on medications! Now, don't get me wrong as what I'm about to say is not meant to have you stop taking your meds. Clearly, if you're a diabetic with a high HgA1c, you need to take your meds. If you have high blood pressure and it is still 146/90, you need your meds. But, this new generation is growing up quickly, diagnosed with ADHD, bipolar, and depression, and placed on medications with very little psychotherapy involvement in their care. Indeed, depression exists. But, when I see a nine-year-old patient in the emergency room on antidepressants, it baffles me. When I hear someone say, "Yes, I did wrong, but it's because I didn't take my medication," I think society has created a new evolution of excuses to approve and justify bad behavior. I believe in behavioral health and the benefits appropriate medications have. However, we must be careful of the reliance we place on meds, so we don't raise a generation who blame their medication non-compliance, rather than their choice, in performing the shocking behavior. In my psychotherapy sessions, I place major emphasis on individual responsibility.

Even psychiatrists can agree. Specifically, I will never forget a case while on a psychiatric rotation of a patient who was diagnosed with Dissociative Identity Disorder, formerly Multiple Personality Disorder. She had been rotated through many popular medications and was maximized on presumably beneficial drugs to treat the disorder, but not one helped her. Finally, the doctor, not wholly religious himself said, "This is out of the realm of meds. There is another factor and source involved in this equation and no medicine can alter this spirit, while altering her dopamine, epinephrine and serotonin balances." There comes a point where it's not the medicine, it's your choice. It's not your brain. It's your spirit. The diagnosis is just that, a diagnosis. Although living with it, you are still an individual with a mind and spirit of your own. Despite a diagnosed body, you have the power to choose to live on with a beautiful, healthy mind and spirit.

There is always a healing that occurs with every diagnosis. Yes, every diagnosis! This is because the healing is that of your spirit and not necessarily of your body. This healing may not take away your physical pain, but it can calm your mind and allow you to keep pushing through until the end. Notice the healing and allow it to take place!

Chapter Six

THROUGH THE MATH

I may be a physician now. And I may also have been a dual-degree student to receive my MBA. But, believe me when I tell you that it was sometimes hard as you know what for me to go to school back in the 1980s and 1990s! So, I don't even have to imagine the difficulties kids and teens face today. I remember the drill quite fondly! Waking up with a fake cough, acting in telling my mom with a slow, groggy voice, "I don't feel good. Do I h-a-v-e to go to school today, Ma?" With that being said, it was always so surprising at the end of the school year, when administrators were giving awards and someone actually received the "Perfect Attendance" award! My friends and I would say, "Wow, goodness grief! How'd they do that when I was counting how many sick days I had left to take off!" Oh, my friends and I were hanging out in the hallways until the bell rang in high school. Then we were hanging out on the campus yard in college, looking fly and people watching. Yep, those were the days! Yet, despite all the drama, my internal focus remained consistent. And, I also had a grandfather who would bang on the table and tell me, "Get that education! You hear me! Knowledge is power!"

My motivation became stronger in college and medical school, but getting over the hump of middle and high school was rough! When you're faced with battles of being laughed at because you actually have your homework done when the teacher asks, getting stares from classmates while raising your hand in class because you actually know the answer, or being teased because you carry a book bag with real books in it, it is easy to call it quits. A concerned person doesn't have to think hard at all when it comes to questioning the high dropout rates in America today. Because when the focus in schools is to increase weapon detectors rather than books and supplies, it's no wonder there's a whole society of kids with beliefs that the system has given up on them.

How does a new generation kid get through math class and ace it, with all the new age drama? When preparation for "back to school" time means making sure you have the latest gear rather than having enough notebooks, how can you make sure that at least the internal focus of learning is present? With all the babies raising babies, how can we assure that parent-teacher associations and parental involvement does not become a thing of the past? Even the so-called ghetto life has become more ruthless, so how can a child keep the desire to be educated? Wouldn't it be nice if we could control our surroundings? It would be real nice if we could change the world and Christians and Muslims would get along, decreasing fears of terror attacks. If the Bloods and Crips would get along, decreasing gangbangs and innocent deaths, wouldn't that be something sweet? And even if more rich people would donate more to the poor so that differences and disparities in American education wouldn't exist, that would be a fine thing. Oh yes, a perfect world would be nice.

But it's hard to change your surroundings. So, you must learn to change yourself. If you've been raised with the thought that knowledge isn't power, change that thought! If you care about what other students will think if you study, stop caring! For real! It was funny one Sunday when Rev. Senator James T. Meeks of Salem Baptist Church of Chicago said, "It's hard out here for brothers cuz they decided to drop out of high school! But it was even harder for older brothers during slavery who witnessed their wives and daughters being raped by white men!"

Ignoring the turning point that occurs, some multiple, is one initial thing students have to get through. So, you're heading in the wrong direction? Trust, that no matter how rough and tough you may be, an event will happen which causes you to question if you're doing the right thing, living the right way. Maybe it's a friend who goes to jail or dies prematurely, a parent who loses a job and you watch them struggle to make ends meet, another student who drops out of school and struggles, or another who chooses an alternative to education and fails. Regardless of the intensity of the situation, there is a turning point moment when we all ask ourselves, "What does math and education have to do with life? Do I really need this?"

For me, it was getting caught cheating with a bunch of friends in ninth grade. It just so happened that one of the members in my crew had a mother who was a teacher. And of course he had the teacher's manual with all the answers. So, the word got around to the rest of us and lo and behold, we cheated. But clearly amateurs, we didn't know how to cheat. I don't remember if we all got perfect scores or what. We weren't the only ones in the class with the answers, but to our luck, four of us were called in to the principal's office and earned detention and a bad reputation for cheating.

Truth is, we were all smart and capable, at a magnet school, but we took advantage of a bad opportunity and got into deep trouble. I took a moment and said, "This is a real trip and how did I get myself in this position?" Contrary to popular belief, it isn't always the crew that makes you do wrong. It isn't always the peer pressure. Many of us know exactly what we are doing, see what we think is an easy way, and run with it. But we don't run into victory, we run straight into a brick wall!!! Boom! At the time, I didn't think teachers would forget that mistake. But, they did. And thank God they saw my hard work and I had another try at learning again and restoring my tarnished reputation. That's because I fought back! I fought back by studying and being focused in class. When someone asked me, "Jerisa, you studied?" I'd say with confidence, "Yep, I ain't playing! Didn't you?" Trust, you can always make a change for the better no matter how deep into a mess you have been!

The phrase, "It happened for a reason," has gotten on my last nerves! We've gotz to stop saying that! When something bad happens in life, someone always says, "Well, it happened for a reason." It's a phrase that keeps you from looking at yourself.

When you lose your job, "It happened for a reason." Not necessarily true! Maybe you didn't work hard enough, had a bad attitude, or were consistently late. When you don't get the job that you wanted you say, "Oh well, it happened for a reason." Well, maybe instead you didn't try hard enough, show dedication enough, pray enough, or weren't likeable enough. When you end up in a bad relationship you again say, "It happened for a reason." Well yeah, the reason is because of your bad choices! When you didn't get the car or house you want you say, "It happened for a reason." Uh, the reason is because you shop too much and your credit is bad! Stop having to place stop payments on checks and put a stop payment on yourself! Trust, I don't excuse myself from any of this. We've all been there. But, we have to get to the point where we can say with certainty, "I've been there and I'm not there anymore. I've changed and more importantly, I've succeeded because of the change. Don't just stop at the thought of things happening for some reason. Try to search and find out what the reason was. Was the reason you? If so, although it may be hard to swallow initially, at least you have a focus that you can work on.

I mention that popular "excuse," I mean phrase, because so many of us look at our situations superficially and fail to see beyond them. If we can only get past the superficial, maybe we can push on to victory, creating our own victory. "*A reason*," keeps us from seeking to understand the "real reason." In a cycle, this keeps us from owning up to the responsibility of control in the situation. Instead of control, we have the "Que sera, sera" attitude…"Whatever will be, will be." After Adam and Eve, we were given free will. So unless you're praying and/or fasting on everything very hard, many of the things that happen are a direct reflection of your choices.

Another way to push through the difficulties surrounding the pursuit of an education is to see yourself beyond the now. Contrary to how gangsters of all races are living, you are not meant to die in your twenties just because you're a poor Black or Hispanic boy/girl! So when you're thirty-something, what will you be doing? Your mom might have been a cashier at Burger King, but you should be progressive and *own* a Burger King! I look at kids today as they're walking home from schools and just think, "It has to be depressing to attend school these days, especially if you want to have a productive and progressive future." Watching

The Oprah Winfrey Show one day, I was alarmed in hearing some educational statistics of the time. Did you know that as of 2007 the United States is no longer the leader in education and that we rank 26 behind poorer countries? How did America allow that to happen? We're actually fighting for "democracy" in Iraq with those rankings? Falling behind in ranks to poorer countries highlights what I will point out later, that it's not always the means you have, but rather the motivation! I was shocked that my home state of Georgia was ranked in the bottom five states for education, with one of the highest dropout rates. Specifically for Blacks, the dropout rate is 50 percent! Even more so, it's still hard to believe that there are schools that look as bad as prisons! But, even well equipped schools have high dropout rates. The show made my own thoughts tangible and it was quite disheartening to actually see the truth I was afraid of realizing. With all the dismal statistics, how do students survive and not only survive, succeed?

In discussing some of the state of American education today with Junior, one of my friends in Atlanta, he said so movingly, "People don't get more by wanting more, they get more by becoming more." When I gave him compliments on the eloquence of the phrase, he said laughingly that he wasn't the author. He believes the author of that meaningful statement is Anthony Robbins. Think about it—simply desiring something will not get you where you want to be. You cannot just possess the desire alone, to have better, as the "to do" attitude of action has to go along with it. While I was becoming the first physician in my family, I didn't have many mentors. Some of the prominent Black physicians published books about their trials after I was already in medical school. And even if there was someone around who'd be willing to share a story, as I'm sure there was, the fear of being rejected over and over with words like, "It's hard and are you sure you wanna do that" was enough to keep my dream wrapped up in a shell for a while. However, what I did have was an inner motivation, a driving thought, "Somebody had to do this before me!"

I was never a fan of history and social studies class, but my attraction to Black history was strong. Even in middle and high school, when I did dramatic presentations, I wanted to act as a slave. Once, for a high school program, I got all dressed up in ragged clothes, a curly wig, and was slow walking with a cane in my hand singing a Negro spiritual! Yeah! If you think that's sad, it isn't. This is because slaves, despite low economics, were high in motivation and had a passion above passions, a determination above determinations. They never received their promised 40 acres and a mule! Yet, they were consistently filled with both desire and do. How is it that they succeeded despite their low means, but kids of today cannot? For me, I saw myself belonging to a people who made something from nothing. And because of that, there was no way I could fail a math class!

There is a different type of slavery that exists today and segregation is still alive and kicking in the good ole' U. S. of A. Some of it is self-inflicted, but the government shouldn't get off that easy without blame, as not all of it is self-inflicted! Affirmative action was not a claim to fame by itself. A fighting spirit went right along with it. It's sad, but poor people have always been expected to succeed with limited resources. Even today, some schools don't have enough computers or fast online services. Some don't have enough books or supplies. Some don't have enough knowledgeable guidance counselors to lead kids into more prominent education and jobs. It's no wonder that according to one Oprah Winfrey show in the spring of 2007, Black and Latino 12th graders are at educational levels equal to white 7th and 8th graders. Thank God there's a recent bill passed to spend one billion dollars modernizing schools. But the results aren't coming quick enough and not to mention, they've been a long time coming!

Another way to get through math is to fear something! Whether it's the fear of failure, fear of being an old dummy, or back in my day, the fear of your parents as well as teachers, fearing something will make you get your study on! When I was in fifth grade, my teacher spanked me. Yes, she took me outside the class, just by the door entryway and using a paddle, gave me a few hard hits. And after it was all over, I had to walk back into class to my chair. All the students could hear it, and some could see it! This was common practice back in the '80s and some teachers did it to students more than others. I really don't remember what I did that day, maybe I talked backed to the teacher, but whatever it was, it had to be something minor, as it didn't take much to bring out the paddle in those days! My mom, like many parents, signed the permission slip giving teachers permission to spank. As a child, you hate being spanked. But years later, you are thankful for the heartfelt correction, which resultantly caused you to fear something, and you're glad the rod was not spared, as it kept you wanting to stay away from misbehaving. Obviously, no school today has teachers who spank, as a parent would be ready to sue and the kids, ready to fight! Even prayer was removed from the system. Some schools don't even say the Pledge of Allegiance because it ends with "...one Nation under God..." Vending machines and metal detectors have been put in place. Do they provide a free and safe feeling? Maybe. But students must also feel at times as though they're going to jail or court, when they walk through those metal detectors. What a turnaround the school system has made.

> For which cause we faint not; but though our outward man perish,
> yet the inward man is renewed day by day...while we look not at the
> things which are seen, but at the things which are not seen:
> for the things which are seen are temporal;
> but the things which are not seen are eternal.
> 2 Corinthians 4:16, 18.KJV

Where you are born makes the difference! Does it now? You're a product of your environment! Are you now? You live in the ghetto, you die in the ghetto! Really now? You live in Bel Air, you stay Bel Air bound! For real now? Wrong! So you're born knowing both parents? While this means you may be more equipped to pass math, your own inner motivation may not be enough. Maybe you don't know your father? While this means you're less advantaged, your internal focus and inner motivation can get you through. You might say, "I wasn't born privileged." Despite this, you have to learn to stop living beneath your privilege and to live by the promise. Stop living by circumstance and live by the Word. This means, that while some thing or some goal may be far from your reach, it is not unreachable. Can't afford books? In this www.com age, who needs books?! It's all online anyway! Don't have a computer? Go to the city's free library! Can't read? Ask the teacher to help you outside of class one day! Stop faking. Stop cheating. And stop being lazy.

So, your parents didn't do anything worthwhile and it may seem as though they don't want *you* to do anything worthwhile? Parents don't always want more for their child, although they should. Even worse, orphans don't have parents. Slaves survived being separated from their families. Get over it and plan to be better than those family members before you. Live in a bad situation, but don't let the bad situation live in you. And, if you think this is impossible, do an online search on Harriet Tubman or W.E.B DeBois. Even Jesus left his parents for greatness at the age of 12! It's not how you start, it's how you finish! It's not what you see, it's what you believe!

Some students respond to fear, and others to expectation. When you fear something or someone, it moves you. Often, the low expectations of others for you, may be enough motivation to succeed. When you have "haters," you have something to work against. My mindset was, "I might have cheated once along with some friends in the ninth grade, but that isn't the real me. And, I might have gotten into a fight in middle school, but that's not the end of me. I might dance and shake my rump like it's hot, but that's not my focus. So, you think I can't do it and you think I'm a product of my environment? Wrong!" You too, have to change your negative life around and make sure that your focus is positive despite your surroundings. And when people doubt you and your abilities, you must be set to tell them, "Well I'm gonna show you! Watch out now!" My motivation back in the early school days was, "I do have something to prove!"

My mom, who believes that each generation should be better than the previous one told me, "No one takes your life, you lay it down." That's a scripture in John, Chapter 10. It has a deep message if you think about it. No one makes you be a big dummy! You may have the hard knock life, but slaves had it worse and still were able to help found civilization, build highways and discover light bulbs.

Truly, when it comes to the hard-knock life, it is difficult and not everyone can live in the ghetto. My mom worked two jobs to keep us out of the ghetto, but she couldn't always keep the lights and water running. The resources in your house may be limited, but don't just see the Internet as a social scene. Who can tell you what you are to do in life? Who can tell you that you're supposed to die in your twenties? Who can call you a big dummy when you study? Trust, life is not meant to be limited. It's even written in the Bible as the Lord said, "I came so that you might have life, and have it more abundantly." Remember this! Don't be fooled into believing in your limitations. Learn the math! Again, it's not how you start, but how you finish!

Why did I choose math as the subject of this chapter on education? Funny enough, I'm sure my high school math teacher isn't asking that question! This is because I almost failed it one semester in the 10th grade. I did say only one semester, because it was a subject that historically was one of my better ones, along with science. But this one semester, I don't really know what happened. It must have been a combination of not studying, not focusing in class, and/or an outside circumstance that caused me to have a bad report card. My mother of course, was upset, not at the teacher, but at me, as again, she was a parent who "didn't play dat"! Some students get C's, D's, and even F's and think they can never work their way back up to A's. But, it is possible. While I can't remember fully the negative trigger that semester, I haven't forgotten voluntarily staying after class daily, to do homework with my math teacher. I don't know the numbers of students that teachers are able to remember during their career, as they have so many. But, there's no way my math teacher could forget me, as I wouldn't let her!

The bad grade motivated me to work harder and motivated me to *show* the teacher that I was working harder. And to teachers who think that staying after school is a waste of time, that same math teacher worked her way right up to being the school principal! I got a bad grade in English once as well, but that one I didn't deserve. Thankfully, my mom had my back, meeting with the teacher every week so he would be on point. When I almost failed Math, she scolded me. When I almost failed English, she did some research and realized that it really wasn't me, and "scolded" the teacher. Either way, parents should be encouraged to get involved in their child's education and want more for them. It's not only the child's future. Contrary to popular belief, when a child fails "math" parents fail to some degree, as well. After that semester, I continued to ace math!

Getting through math means getting over the hype! Video Soul and Atari was the hype back in my day. Today, the hype is "106 and Park" and Play Station! Boy, did I love to dance and play "Pac Man" on my computer! I would come home and be glued to Video Soul, at least on those sporadic months when we could afford cable! And the best gift my grandfather gave me was a computer program with the Pac Man game on it! I would stay up late playing that game some nights! My mom didn't let me go to very many parties. Dating? She wasn't too fond of teenagers doing that either. But in school, on pep rally days, myself and other students would show off our dance routines that we worked so hard to choreograph. And despite my love of dancing, booty dancing, I knew how to answer those mathematical differential equations! Wanting at one point during college to be a model, like Tyra Banks? Maybe. But my desire was not to be a stripper. I did not really want to be labeled as a video girl, although it crossed my mind a few times. Funny enough, even some video girls today don't want to be video girls!

Furthermore, what is it about hip-hop that controls Black folk, but not the white counterparts who actually purchase the music more? Even if you are "Sweet Sixteen," why can't the dirty dancing stop at the dance floor? Why does it have to continue to the bedroom, with the possibility of children conceiving a child? I know, it's commonly stated that Blacks live hip-hop and experience it, while the other ethnicities have the rich houses and the well-equipped schools and make mockery of the music. But goodness grief, Blacks have always had to work harder! Nothing good has ever come easy. Historically, minorities have lived and succeeded despite a particular environment. So if others can turn it (hip-hop) off, Blacks need to learn how to as well! Ya dig?

Quick fix seekers die without a purpose! My grandfather, a math teacher until his retirement, used to take his index finger, point to and touch my forehead and tell me, "What you get up here, no one can take away!" There are so many excuses for not getting an education. One commonly heard is, "There are many successful people without college degrees!" This is true. But the value of a high school education is limitless and should not be underestimated. True, Bill Gates dropped out of Harvard University. But this is a top Ivy League University! Dropping out of Harvard means the educational foundation was laid and deeply rooted in him from high school. True, P. Diddy dropped out of Howard University. But by then, he had enough courses underneath his belt. Think about it, if these successful men did not value education, they wouldn't be two of the largest contributors to improving education, right?

There have been a few individuals I've helped get into medical school and the advice that I feel best in giving them is, "Sacrifice. It may be a few years of your life, but it's just a few years. Make the short-term sacrifice for a long-term benefit." Instead of asking students where they see themselves in just five years, we should ask them where they see themselves when they're 30, or at what age would they want to retire. Students, you don't want to look back when you're forty-something and say, "If I'd only gone to math class." Get it while the getting is good, as they say. You won't be a teenager or in your twenties for long. So pick up the book, search education online, ask the teachers for help, and attempt to do your homework even when you don't have a parent to ask about it. Desire to be better! Study to be better!

I was disheartened to read in a 2006 issue of Howard University's Alumni Magazine that the Black male college population had decreased during and since the 1990s. High school guidance counselors need to be equipped with the knowledge in distributing college information to both college-prep students and to those who don't "appear" college bound. It makes a difference when you know that when you study, there is money and financial aid out there. Even if you have to fund your entire education through loans, statistics show that a college graduate applying for the same job as a non-college graduate will have a better salary. Though being a pain at times, you will be able to make payments on your loan. You will be independent and self-sufficient. Furthermore, if you decide to go even higher with income potential, by pursuing specific careers or business adventures, making those payments will be even easier.

College and career counselors also need to be well informed and ready to deliver all of the options that exist. Even I, at Howard, had to do a little research on my own in applying to medical school, as at the time, my pre-med advisor didn't know much about osteopathic physicians. All the information I received was about allopathic medical schools. This could be a reflection of the much lesser number of schools, as osteopathic physicians are doctors indeed, and great ones at that. Students, you may receive limited information from folk, but trust me there are many ways to reach your dream. So, don't be so accepting of what you hear. Do your own research!

I briefly spoke earlier about students being determined enough to get educated, and to study despite a lack of parental involvement. While many are concerned, surprisingly many parents aren't involved. I remember an episode of "Good Times" when the character Michael, in middle school at the time, started at a better and predominantly white school. He had to travel to school via many bus changes, as it wasn't in his low-income neighborhood. It could be this lodged in my memory because of the many reruns I've seen, but also because his mother and father were quite hard on him, stern voices difficult to forget. When Michael didn't want to study, they made him pick up a book and showed him the importance of doing so. The expression on his father's face said, "Boy, you must be crazy. You want me to hurt you?" They questioned when he came home without a homework assignment and did not let him get off easy. Even his brother and sister were involved in his education, truly exhibiting a family affair.

Today, there's less of that. Many parents are so involved in their own well-being and satisfaction that they neglect a child's hidden cry for help. So many single mothers are searching to find a father for their child, forgetting that for many years single moms have successfully raised children. Parents, ask your children about their homework. If you did not graduate from high school, do your best with your child to make sure he/she does. We should want better for our children. Furthermore, there are many churches now providing programs, so consider getting your own GED. Math concepts don't change, but as time has passed, hopefully your motivation to do them has.

As I write this chapter, despite the disparities that exist in education, despite the changed focus exhibited by some students, and despite the increase in school violence, I smile in pride and hope, as minorities are holding some powerful positions, not just in the United States, but also in the world. Because I liked President Bill Clinton's leadership manner, I don't have much to say about President George W. Bush. However, as far as Bush's staff...wow! Talk about ethnic diversity! Wow! Colin Powell was the United States of America Secretary of State. Condoleezza Rice was in charge of the United States of America National Security, before being appointed as Secretary of State. Alberto Gonzalez was the U.S. Attorney General. Kofi Annan was the United

Nations General. And to top all that, Senator Barak Obama was able to unify millions during his quest for Presidency in 2008. Minorities may just hold a few powerful positions in comparison to other ethnicities, but they are powerful indeed. Moreover, whether Republican or Democrat, the power is equivocal. Trust, that these powerful world leaders studied their math! Affirmative action or not, becoming qualified was not something they took lightly!

The system may be against you, but take on the challenge. It may seem hard as you know what, but it's been done before under even more strenuous circumstances. When getting an education is not the current hype, forget the hype. When your crew laughs or attempts to discourage, tell them nicely, "I'll see you at the reunion!" Prepare yourself for a life of longevity and success. Take the world by storm! Brainstorm!

Chapter Seven

THROUGH
THE INTERVIEW

You know, it can be quite a difficult decision, and all women can relate, picking out an interview suit. It has to be one of the hardest things, answering the following questions: Which color to wear? Should it be a pantsuit or a skirt? And if a skirt, what length should it be? What accessories, if any, do you wear? Oh, and the shoes! You just cannot forget about the shoes! For a man, lucky for them, the decision seems to be centered on just a couple of questions: What color shirt? What kind of tie? And, God forbid you know someone who works where you're applying or you know there's been a group of interviewees before you! In this case, you've struck platinum in finding someone who will ultimately become your victim of harassment with endless questioning! There's no doubt you're ready to flood them with questions like: "What are people generally wearing? What color is popular? What type suit seems to impress the boss?" After probably a bit too much research, you've purchased the suit, laid out the appropriate jewelry, and picked the shoes. But you're not done yet. Just before the day arrives, you recognize that the hair has to be in tip-top shape! Gotta look good from head to toe, you know! So now, and also to catch up on the latest gossip, you've scheduled an appointment with your favorite barber or hair stylist who you know will hook the head up. Yes, appearance is everything and you have that prepared and wrapped up in a bag! You're ready now…looking absolutely fabulous! Yeah, you definitely look the part! You're so confident they are going to love you, immediately draw up a contract, and have you sign on the dotted line before you leave the interview! Really now?

People always ask each other, regardless of age, "What do you want to be when you grow up?" Now, why it's asked to kids as young as five years old, I couldn't tell ya. But everyone is expected to be able to name something, even if they do change their mind thirty times! As a medical student, I can't tell you how many times I heard the question asked to me or to someone around me, "Are you sure you want to be a physician? It's not too late to change your mind, you know." And you can't forget about the popular interview question, "Where do you see yourself in five years?" That's one people really can't get enough of! You're almost certain to have to answer that one during an interview! This fascination with the type of work a person will do sheds significant light on the importance of finding and establishing purpose. Probably doing this early on would be most beneficial. Purpose is something that cannot be concealed no matter how good you look in that interview suit, honey. Well actually, it can be disguised, but eventually if you're in a position where your heart is not, the cover-up is only short term. So you're interviewing for a job, dressed to kill, but is it the right interview, the right one for you? That is the dreaded, but real question to be answered; more so than what color interview suit you should wear!

I met a man who worked at an advertising company for many years. He worked there seemingly since he was of age to work anywhere! Everyone knew he would most likely be there until the company closed its doors! Although he worked there for over 20 years, in his heart he knew there was something else he was *supposed* to be doing. This man, who happens to be a Black man, decided he wanted to start a business and thus came up with a creative, productive, easily million-dollar idea and is currently jump-starting his own business. He is having some difficulty, but he's confidently jumping through the hoops. Where you work now may be a means to an end, but how do you know that your current career is what you're supposed to be doing until the end? Is there something else, some other idea that has been idle and unattended? Could it be that this idea is just waiting to sprout? Well, of course you know that it's never too late. And if you've already retired from a position, that's almost perfect, as you have plenty of time to water a new idea and get it into motion! Retirement is not an excuse. If you don't use those brain cells, they atrophy (get smaller)!

We all have a purpose. Some have multiple purposes. Although frequently thought of as existing in careers, everyone's purpose is not placed in what type of work they do. You could be interviewing for a position as an Administrative Assistant, as you've done that type of work before. You may very well love it and do it well. But, when you pray and desire a purposeful life, there's possibly something outside of the daytime job that you should be accomplishing. Maybe you work as a security guard, but there's someone you should tutor? Or maybe you're a computer programmer, but art is your passion? Or perhaps you're currently an athlete, but you realize a desire for community service? The first thing we must realize as we interview for jobs is not to lock ourselves into one position. Too commonly, you find a job, work arranged hours, and go home, only to get up the next day to do the same routine. When you actively seek your purpose, becoming fixated in a position isn't an option. It just isn't!

There's a difference between a job and a purpose. Many people say that you choose a job based on interests. If you like horoscope, you may seek to be an astronomer or palm reader. If you love protecting, you may seek to be a security guard. Even in selecting what type of physician, medical students are frequently given personality profiles to help guide them into the decision. I'm not sure how closely we actually follow those personality guides. But, definitely to a large degree, we choose our specialty. Contrarily, accomplishing our purpose doesn't necessarily mean doing what *we* want. You don't necessarily choose your purpose. That's why it's so difficult to obtain, because first, you have to figure out what your purpose is. There may or may not be an interview for reaching your purpose. Furthermore, if there is an interview, you probably don't have to go overboard in figuring out what to wear, as the whole process should flow naturally.

I remember when my mother, in her 50s, began tutoring an elementary school student. There are people in there 20s and 30s who don't even tutor and here she is doing it? In my opinion, I said to myself, "She works all day, is studying herself, barely has time for leisure, and is tutoring?" But, sure enough, that student went from being an "F" student to a straight "A" student and was soon accepted into a highly rated high school! Purpose does not necessarily come along with your regular job duties and even appears to be directly outside the mainstream of your desires. However, it is nonetheless fulfilling. Purpose may also be sacrificial. Contrary to job duties, which may or may not offer you solace and a sense of accomplishment, establishing and doing your purpose(s) always makes you feel good. It's interesting how you pick a job that you want, interview for it and may or may not ultimately enjoy it. Yet, while you don't always choose a purpose, when you accomplish it, it is always rewarding! Purpose, in my opinion, is also different from the feeling of "living a dream." When you feel that you are "living your dream," this of course, is something you want. This feeling comes when you've not only reached your goal, but did so beyond your initial imagination. It's like you're living larger than life now! My point is, purpose is not at all times locked into what our wants are. A job is a means to an *end*. Living a dream means you're living *beyond* your perceived tangible end. But a purpose is a means to a *beginning* for you or for someone else.

As stated, purpose is not necessarily a choice. So many people pray for direction, but still add their own two cents into the matter. For example, some might say, "Lord, I'll go wherever you want me to go, as long as California, warm, sunny weather and beaches are in the picture." Basically, what you're telling God is, "I'll accept what you want, as long as it is in line with what I want, too." That's not how it works! You should be in total submission to God and His way in order to reap the full benefits of what he has for you.

When you're searching for a job position or to establish your purpose, be aware that the door may slam in your face. This is OK. However, it isn't OK when you refuse to knock on the door. Be encouraged to knock. Knock! If it doesn't open right away, keep knocking. Yet, when you knock, make sure you are well prepared for the position behind the door, or at least have some eagerness to learn. I remember eating at a restaurant when a girl walked in and said, "I see the Help Wanted sign. Can I have an application?" One of the employees responded nicely, "We don't have applications, but we accept resumes." The girl stood there, didn't move nor reply. When the owner also greeted her, because she looked a bit awkward just standing there, he said the same thing. He answered just as the employee did. This time, the girl said with a little attitude, "I have a resume, but it's not updated." In this case, the owner was put into a difficult situation, especially with the young lady's composure, so he simply said, "Well, just give us what you have." He could easily have said, "Come back when you have a current resume." Of course, she didn't get a call back. I said to myself, "How do you go looking for a job without an updated resume and then get an attitude when the owner acts nonchalant? Are they supposed to be left to figure out what's accurate on your resume, like your address and telephone number?" Really, think about this!

Preparation should not be taken lightly. In this case, being prepared could not only have made the difference between getting hired or not—it likely meant much more than that! When you go job-hunting, preparation and presentation can determine what position you will be placed in, whether you're a cashier or deserving of a higher position. You may have just enough experience to be a cashier, but how you reveal yourself that particular day could automatically place you in a position for a natural promotion. Whenever you go to apply or interview for a position, keep in the back of your mind a level up from what you're actually applying for. Make room for an increase at the beginning!

The night before an important interview with a residency position, I received bad news. Isn't it funny how bad news knows just when to get delivered? At the time, my grandfather was losing his eyesight. I remember having to console my mother, and my grandfather, whom I had never heard cry, until that night. This I had to deal with after calling my dad and a friend, Denise, along the way, driving from Pennsylvania to Illinois for the interview, to send me some money via Western Union. Going to medical school broke, when most everyone else my age was making some sort of salary, isn't comforting. Nonetheless, I looked at maps to locate cities where I could take a break and where they could wire the money. I remember when my friend said, "Gary, Indiana? What in the world are you doing out there"?! A budgeted medical student, I had always been traveling the last two years of medical school, as I lived in whatever housing the hospitals were providing. So, it was constantly funny when a friend or family member would ask, "So where are you *now*?"

It can be very difficult preparing for an interview when you're broke. Seriously! In these types of cases, you're not concerned about what you are going to wear; you just want to get there, just show up for goodness sake! But I've spoken with people who did buy that "interview suit" as a big investment, likely the only decent threads they have. They stated that it added a bit of confidence to the process. Not only was I broke and collecting tickets from all the pay tolls I couldn't pay, but the news of my grandfather and the tears I heard him cry brought tears to my own eyes. I woke up on interview morning all puffy-eyed and still having to drive another two hours to the hospital. But when I arrived, I put my game face on and my best foot forward. Before that day, I had met a bunch of other interviewees who interviewed at the same program and who were full of advice. To my surprise, mine was nothing like theirs. All of my pre-interview research and the information I had received about the interview was not true and of no use in my case! I approached the door expecting that the interview would be just me and the Program Director; instead I walked into a conference room full of people! How did I get so *lucky*? Panel interviews can be challenging, trying to make sure you divide your eye contact appropriately. But, they liked me, and I was set to rock and roll, at least for a bit.

It's true, "You never know what a day will bring." And, "Practice makes perfect." Until I started my job, I never really dealt with close friends and family members being sick. I've learned in the process that the more things you are forced to face, the more you can deal with. You get to a point where as they say, "You've cried so many tears, you can't cry anymore." But, initially, it was a hard transition. Likewise, with young adults just starting jobs, or possibly even starting school far away from home, the adjustment period can be difficult for some, no matter how strong you've been in the past. Maybe in your case, it's not sickness, but other personal issues, or maybe it's tough competitors at your workplace. But, it's important to note the distracters early on and seek help so you don't position yourself badly to lose the job.

You never know a good thing until it's gone. In my case, the day I was told I would no longer be contracted with my residency position was a pretty bad one, just a few days shy of my thirtieth birthday. First of all, despite some previous mistakes in how I handled scheduling during bad times, I had put that behind me and was trucking along well, so I thought. Second of all, how it was presented to me in the center of a hospital cafeteria, for all onlookers to see, was absolutely embarrassing. And third, I had been going through personal issues, including domestic battery, and was doing my best to succeed despite the situation. Nonetheless, it was a dim and pitiful day. I couldn't even stand, but thank God, there were angels amongst the onlookers, who carried me, took me into their offices, consoled and prayed with me, and inspired me. Ultimately, the decision was based mostly on incorrect information. Moreover, due to distractions at the time, I wasn't completely at my best, so I was preparing myself to appeal. Yet, to my surprise two days later, without needing to appeal, the decision was reversed. It was a wake up call for me, and in combination with other struggles I had recently survived, it only made me stronger, and my testimony livelier.

There was a lot of praying...a whole lot. If I ever doubted my career choice, no matter how good a physician some say I am, when it was taken from me and immediately, easily given back, there was nothing further to doubt. What's for you is for you. Even if you make a mistake, if God has it for you, no one can take it away. However, when something similar happens to you, a layoff or a termination, there is a sense of courage in despair that exists, which is hard to grasp on to at the moment. Thus, if you can hold on and believe, you will watch the situation turn around for you, without even having to fight the battle. I heard it stated once, "When one door closes, another opens." And let me add that you don't have to knock the door down!

Certainly, I must address the issues that can move us into positions we don't want or even need to be in. Some jobs will understand family illness and leaves of absences, some will not. You're going to have to search yourself and decide if you can adapt to certain industry demands. Again, if you pray, and if it is for you, you will have it. But, there are things you can prevent. For me, I didn't tell people at work what was going on in my personal life. I let them think whatever they wanted as I thought it was "my business, not theirs." But, this is not always how you should handle a tough time that is likely causing you to fall short on your job duties. By the time I had taken control, it obviously was a little too late, and I still had to disclose my recent experiences, after being told of termination in the middle of a cafeteria! So, I encourage you to not only take control of what distracts you, but inform the powers that be, as well. You may be tactful in not telling them, but rest assured, they may not consider being tactful in telling you that you're fired!

One cannot talk about interviews and jobs without speaking of your coworkers. It would be just lovely if we all worked at such a place where everyone got along all the time. I saw a documentary once on television about the Google compound and how peaceful and accommodating it is. I thought "Wow, that's a real comfortable place to work!" And I truly believe it is. However, most people are not blessed with that sort of ease. Actually, I say it would be nice, but jobs without some conflict and drama can be a little dull at times, you know. After all, the best dramas win Oscar and Tony awards! Nonetheless, in some high-powered markets and industries, competition is a natural phenomenon. Many probably would not exist if there were no competitors! There wouldn't be a race to the top to be partner in a large law firm, or vice-president of a distinguished department. It's commonly stated, "Make your haters your motivators." What a great way to put your competitors in perspective. Yes, when it comes to competitors, you have to keep an eye on them. Don't worry about them, but keep an eye.

I remember talking to one person while he traveled on conference with a few of his coworkers who were competing against him for research grants. They had to sleep in the same hotel room, despite really needing to focus their minds and practice their upcoming presentations. I told him laughingly, "Now when you go to sleep tonight, close one eye to rest, but make sure you keep the other one open so you can see what's going on with your competitive roommates!" The next day, he jokingly said he tried to do it, but of course he knew it was a figure of speech. Seriously, staying steps ahead means seeking to know what your competitor will do before they can even think of doing it.

When competition goes bad, it can get really bad. Sometimes people who see you as a threat, will deliberately convey information that is entirely wrong or unconfirmed. Don't you just hate that! I experienced this once, and after taking moments to calm my initial annoyance, I was able to seek steps to have the controversy corrected. At the same time, it's funny how two people in the same situation can perceive differently of what's actually going on. You may have the best intentions, but become misunderstood and ultimately misinterpret another, only leading to more and more confusion and frustration; and lo and behold, you've gotten yourself into an unnecessary argument. No matter how innocent you were at the start this is badly perceived. The end can be quite unpleasant, so on-the-job arguments are never beneficial. Learn to take a deep breath and walk away. I'm practicing this myself. If the issue needs to be addressed, maybe do so once you've re-evaluated the situation again.

Furthermore, your competitors want to see you upset, arguing. Once you've done that you have succeeded only in receiving their negative energy. You may have just lost ground with your boss, as well. Once they upset you, you can no longer actively and diligently do your job. At that moment, and however long it takes you to "get it together," you are not a competitor of theirs. You, now have issues! They now on the other hand, can use your "therapeutic" time to gain ground!

I remember getting advice once from an unlikely colleague who really is a master in his field. I can't help but mention it here because it was really good, and actually a funny way to look at conflict on the job. He had received the advice himself once when he was in the center of a dispute at work. When you're in disagreement with someone or trying to figure out how to get over the dispute, you can't let them know it got to you or that it affected you in any way. You must shake their hand, but after shaking their hand go right into the bathroom and wash your hands off if you desire. He could've meant this literally or figuratively. I took the comment figuratively. However, if you really despise your colleague, even their touch, I guess you'd be one to really go and wash your hands. Hopefully, it's not *that* bad. Figuratively, this means put a smile on the outside, roll your eyes on the inside.

97

Know that they're probably doing the same thing when they see you...funny enough! Do this until you've healed yourself of that negative energy. The confusion may never be settled, but that negative energy can and should dissipate over time.

After talking about purpose versus job, the search, preparedness, personal conflict, and competitors, there's just one more thing I'd mention right now. When it comes to jobs and advancement, nothing is more gratifying and moving to me at least, than to see someone age 40 and up, either return to school or make a career change for the better. I have so much respect for those individuals who have worked a job for some time, and ultimately decide to obtain an even higher education, open a business, or engage in some other advancement. I've personally met many taking on that pathway, and I've seen the difficulties they face. These include having to take national board exams where their score is averaged against the 20-something year olds; or having to color their gray hair for interviews when others are fashionably far from needing Botox. Not to meaningfully mention my mom and Botox in the same paragraph, but in her fifties, she completed a doctoral program in education. I also have colleagues who finished medical school in their late forties. This is very admirable.

So what happens to a dream deferred? If you don't settle during your course of job seeking, that dream eventually becomes a realization. If you don't have a goal you want to reach, you are truly placing yourself at a life disadvantage, aimlessly wandering around on earth, simply occupying space.

If you interview and get the job you want, good for you! You made it and your hard work has paid off! But continue to grow as 10 years from the first day at the job, you may find yourself wanting something entirely different and new. So go for it and don't stop! If you interview and get the job you really don't want, one of those interim positions, hang in there! Don't settle in when the bills are getting paid and say, "Well, I'm doing OK. I'm making ends meet." Ready yourself for that next interview. Get more training or meet more people. Don't make a home on that stepping stone. Get ready to climb higher! If you interview and don't get a job at all, don't give up! Knock on a different door, maybe an entirely separate job market. If you're not offered an interview, re-evaluate yourself and consider that there is obviously some other position or place/location out there for you. After all the preparation for the actual interview, be reminded of a possible and distinct purpose, be mindful of personal issues and distractions and how to manage them, keep your competitors in your thoughts, and ultimately keep re-evaluating yourself and never settle! Your retirement does not have to be your last day of work. Most importantly, your being and end is not based on your 401K. Happy interviewing!

Chapter Eight

THROUGH
THE LOVE

Just because you have something in common with someone that alone, doesn't mean he/she is *your* someone! And just
because you believe in the theory of "opposite attraction" does not
mean you should ignore the fact that the person is really getting on
your last nerves!

I will never, ever, ever forget a patient encounter while
doing a hospital rotation in Atlanta, Georgia. At a pediatric clinic,
an 11-year-old little girl visited for a regular checkup. Although
her age was 11, she looked all of like a girl getting ready to
graduate high school, ready to vote! Despite her age, she wasn't
shy at all. Rather, she seemed quite open, so although initially
shocked with a nurse's question to the patient, her demeanor
helped me understand.

Before I entered the room, I took a quick look through the
chart and was prepared to examine an 11-year-old little girl. The
nurse and I entered the room and all of a sudden, while obtaining
the girl's blood, the nurse asked her, "Do you have sex?" A
medical student at the time, I said to myself, "I hadn't thought to
ask *her* that question!" To my surprise, the little girl said without
any shame and with a smile, "Yeah." She was so excited that she

could say yes to that question! All I could say was, "Hmm." Immediately after the first question, the nurse really shocked me by taking it a step further. She didn't ask any medical questions about protection or birth control, she went straight to the biggy! She asked the little girl, "Have you ever had an orgasm?" I took a step back, swallowed the "lump" in my throat, and said to myself, "OK, wait a minute, did she just ask this 11-year-old little girl if she has orgasms? Naaw, she didn't do that!" But again, the girl in ever so much excitement, said, "Yep!" I remember the look the nurse and I gave each other after hearing that yes, as though to say, "She's got to be kidding us, right?" It was as though the world stopped for a minute. I'm sure she was thinking what I was thinking which was, "I know people who've been in love and married for years, who haven't had an orgasm!!"

Of course, the nurse took it a little further, as she had to verify the little girl's definition of an orgasm by asking her if she knew what it was. She said sort of firmly and sort of jokingly, "How do you know what an orgasm is young lady?" The girl returned a looked to the nurse as though she was offended by the question and as though the nurse was crazy and said, "Of course I know what an orgasm is, don't you?" I gulped my laugh! I thought, "Here it is, an 11-year- old little girl getting ready to give us explicit details?" I was speechless, and still wanting to believe I was dreaming, I went on with my history-taking and exam. This little girl was definitely no little girl! But, what did she really know about orgasms? Well, I hate to burst her bubble now, but little girl if you're reading this, you knew nothing about orgasms, sex, or love. You're not making love, you're play-loving. And speaking of *love*, why didn't we ask her about *it*?

Flee youthful lusts: but follow righteousness, faith, charity, peace.
2 Timothy 2:22.KJV

I'm not an expert on love, but I have taken note of a few things. In writing this chapter, I must admit even though at one point it was almost finished, I stumbled and had to take an extended break. Experiencing a lustful relationship myself got a little in the way. Yet when that experience ended, it's amazing how the words began to flow. It's funny how society has taught us to grade love today, quite differently, interestingly enough, from how our grandparents and great grandparents did. Back in the day, they had that sort of fighting love, the "I would do anything to make it work love;" the love that never ceased, the love that dealt little with physical and more with inner self, the hard to break and surviving love, that simple love. Today, girls and guys of the "nip and tuck" generation are less concerned about an inner self, not even really caring to know what it is. Love today has three measures: money, sex, and orgasm. While there are three measures, there are so many types of love! Nowadays, we have conditional, divisive, quick-to-anger, and temporary love, the you-betta-not-do-anything-wrong type of love. It's common to hear a "happily" married man's girlfriend say, "I love him because he treats his wife so good." Note that his girlfriend is *not* his wife. It's common to hear men say, "She dropped it like it was hot. That's why I love her." There's the hurting type of love, also called "hard" love. There's the you-love-me-so-I'll-love-you love, the right now love, the I'm-gonna-sex-you-until-you're-addicted love, the pregnancy-induced love, the no-matter-how-little-time-I-spend-with-you-you'll-always-be-there-waiting love, the I'm-gonna-marry-you-now-and-hope-I-grow-to-love-you-later love, the I-can't-find-no-one-else-so-you'll-just-have-to-do love, and the lists go on! I can't keep up with them! With so many conditions, you have to ask, "What's love got to do with all of this?" I mean, really?

We've even found ways to cover love as though it doesn't exist or is some abnormal terminology. Think about this. When did the statement, "I'm *in love* come about?" How many times have you heard, "I love him, but I'm not *in love* with him." Huh? People even pronounce the two differently when they speak, placing greater emphasis on the "in love" part. Many times, I denied love and spoke of the difference in loving someone, yet not being *in love* with them. Society has taught us to firmly and causatively differentiate the two. "I love my baby momma, but I'm *in love* with the girl I'm dating." "I love my husband, but I'm *in love* with my other boy toy." Say what? I mean, was this *in love* terminology written anywhere in the good book, also known as The Bible? Have you ever read, "God was so *in love* with the world, he gave his only begotten son…?" No, because the term is a societal one. It has become acceptable and is the cause of considerable confusion, chaos, division, and breakups.

With so many definitions and types, who really knows what love is anyway? We've gotten away from the scriptural references of love. We've learned to associate love with neglect, and our desire to believe that love endures hardship has been taken to an entirely different level! I've heard people's stories and even have a few of my own. A person I thought I was in love with treated me with disrespect over and over again. Vulnerable and desiring to be loved, I allowed it. I knew I wasn't supposed to be with him, but I followed my flesh and became blind! This man, who was much older than me at the time, insulted my virginity, insulted my character, only to apologize by sending me a huge flowering plant. I shouldn't have taken him back after that, but of course I did. You know how we women can love some flowers! It's interesting to speak with people who hate love or deny it so much, as though it doesn't exist! Granted, sometimes it can be where a person is in a situation, being in love with the idea of love, rather than in love with the person. This happens quite often and if you can realize it early on—that you love the idea of love more so than that person—you can save yourself quite a bit of drama.

Denying love may also be a comfort, an escape-goat when you reflect and try to justify your behavior. You want to believe you weren't in love. But honey, if you gave that person your heart and made them the center, you were indeed, in love. Although you may think you're not in love or don't know what love is, this is not necessarily so! If you've ever been in a situation where you know he doesn't want to see you, but you still want to see him, you just might be in love. If you know he's sleeping around and you still want to have sex with him, you just might be in love. If she treats you like a punk, and you still want to be with her, you just might be in love. If you know she likes your money, and you still want to be with her, you just might be in love. If you said, "Yeah, that's me" to any of the above, you simply can't deny love. It might not have been a "real" love, but it was definitely one of the kinds of love, a caught-up-in the moment type of love. Getting through this topic of love, let's travel from good to bad, as that love-like lust usually starts off that way, right?

Love feels great! It's one of the few vulnerable feelings we accept! I never understood why the cloud had to be number nine, but it sure feels great floating on it! When you love a person, although they may make mistakes and treat you badly, in your mind they can do no wrong. Even if you fear love, you can't escape it, nor do you desire to, in most cases. Although I'm speaking of love of the opposite sex, the greatness of love is universal. If you love chocolate, you feel great when you it eat. The nerves in your body rumble from head to toe. If you love material things, you feel like a king/queen when you shop. You may end the shopping spree broke, but you're smiling in the fitting room, trying on all those clothes. And loving yourself, well you can reach a point where you do that too much. But it too, makes you feel remarkable! The great feeling you have while thinking, "I'm the bomb" can however, turn into egotistical behavior. Too much love of these things turns it from being great, into being harmful. You can eat too much chocolate and become unhealthy, you can shop until you're broke, and you can love yourself until you're selfish! So you can love stuff and people too much and when it gets to the point where it consistently hurts, it's time to re-evaluate!

Love is a gamble. Let's look at an example with black-jack. You think you have a good person, a good hand. So you play a bet or you share some love. The dealer deals, and guess what, you win this time! Good for you! Next, the person you love makes a boo-boo, or you get a bad hand. Dealer deals and to your surprise, you win again. This time it's because you decided to love the person in spite of their wrong. Wonderful! Yet, the person makes another boo-boo, you get a bad hand. Again, you decided to yield. This time, L-O-S-E-R! You lost time and money. But, you don't give up, you continue loving the person and playing with those bad hands, thinking almost miraculously you'll win. But, the dealer deals and more mistakes are made by the person. You lose more money and more time. One would think you would decide to quit this time and fold. But no, not yet! You don't care about your cycle of losing, nor the damage it is doing to you. So the dealer deals you a bad hand, the person continues to hurt you. Sometimes, you ultimately win and sometimes you ultimately lose. Sometimes, in order for love to come out on top, you must let go. Even if you get the person in the end, was it worth all of the trouble? I can't answer that as, to each his/her own. If you've found perfect love on earth, you don't have to go *through* it. Some are not intended to find great love on earth. Scripture tells us the greatest and first love is not here! But, if you're in a bad cycle of love, it's time to regroup and get ready for a new love. Don't be easily swayed or you will fall for tricks. I learned that if you delay the ending, you increase the hurt and delay the healing!

Take some time and ask yourself, "What would I do for love?" Would you have sex for love, get pregnant for love, break the law for love, do drugs for love, deny yourself for love, beg for love? Would you marry someone you don't love, hoping that love will come *after* marriage? Or maybe you're the type who feels nothing needs to be done to obtain love. Then ask yourself, "What will I accept for love?" Would you be tricked for love, be ignored for love, be abused for love? With all the specifications surrounding love, it's no wonder the youth of today have it all mixed up and backwards. I wonder if they even know the "K-I-S-S-I-N-G" song that my friends and I sung growing up. You know the one, "Amy and Chris, sitting in a tree, K-I-S-S-I-N-G. First comes love, then comes marriage, then comes Amy with the baby carriage." If they know the beat or rhythm, they've certainly changed the sequence! Nowadays, the baby comes well before the love or marriage, if love (or marriage) comes at all.

Love is a union! It is common to refer to the term "soul mate" when one thinks of joining with another. People differ on whether there is this one-of-a-kind individual or if multiple "soul mates" can be encountered throughout life. We've all heard the statistics. Fifty percent of marriages end in divorce. Although, I recently heard that the percentage may actually be less, as fewer people are choosing to get married. Like many things we hear from society, we've unfortunately grown to accept divorce no matter how diffusible the cause might have been. When the marriage gets rocky, rocky being exemplified as one or two arguments, many are quick to seek a divorce attorney! Have you ever wondered whatever happened to the sanctity in marriage? Some people think that love exists in numbers, not realizing that STDs and babies are more probable. Premarital sex ultimately leads an individual to comparison. Because of that, infidelity is sadly ordinary. I've heard, "She's not a freak, so I can't marry her." Or, "He doesn't know how to plant it, so I can't marry him." Today, I personally know women who date "happily" married men as though marriage means "man more available"! There used to be a time when "happily" married men sought single women by hiding their wedding ring. Now, they don't have to! The ring has become a natural magnet for some women saying to them, "Go get 'em girl!" Despite this, many single women who date "happily" married men really want to be married themselves one day! I wish that if the women can't see the harm they are doing to the married families and children, at least they might notice the harm they do to themselves. What goes around comes back around again. It really does! While singles experiencing intimacy with a "happily" married person may be freaky and exciting to some, you'll never have all of someone else's spouse, because he or she is not fully available to the single. Note, I distinguish "happily" from "unhappily" married folks undergoing a divorce. Learn to want more for yourself!

If you're seeking to be in a love union, know that you should not live your life through your husband or wife. When you do this, temporary happiness is all that is obtained. Marrying someone else does not satisfy your purpose. When you get married, you should be asking each other, "What's our purpose together?" Your purpose is separate from him/her. It may not be completely accomplished, but at least think about it before you unite. Contrary to popular belief, someone else does not complete you! Rather, they should compliment you. You are a whole person now, even in your singularity. Even the Bible says that marriage is not for everyone and ultimately removes a part of you from God. When you die, no one is going to be saying, "She was so good/bad in life because she was married to so and so." God will not be judging you based on who you chose for your wife. While getting over someone whom I thought was my first love, one of my best friends, Ndidi, helped me remember that even when you give your heart to someone and unite, God has to remain the center.

Love is sexy! When it comes to love, it's no secret that the opinions and actions of men and women differ. I think girls, while some deny a desire for love, still want to feel special in a guy's mind, but the "special" is subject to clarification in the "nip and tuck" generation! Special, today means being "the number one girl, the main chick in a set of women." Special today, means doing whatever is necessary, even though you feel you shouldn't. Many girls growing up today sell their body for either money or reputation, in search of love. And if it's not for love, it's so they feel "highly regarded." They opt for breast implants because it makes them "feel" better about themselves when it attracts whistle blows from boys. Plastic surgery can be very beneficial when done for the right reasons—not to achieve negative attention from the opposite sex. Contrarily, many men look for relationships being controlled by orgasms. Somehow, society has taught us that when it comes to sex and being sexy, love doesn't matter. Since when did love and sex not mix? In the case with the young patient described earlier in this chapter, we didn't ask her if she had ever loved. But, I bet at least to that question, her answer would be no!

While love is sexy, it's not flashy. Girls today have been taught to love their bodies, lessen their inner spirit, and use that bodily love to gain love from someone else. They are told in many song lyrics to get their bodies tight and right, to drop it like it's hot, and to loose booty! Young girls today haven't learned to separate bad lyrics from existence, as my friends and I did dancing to similar lyrics. Girls have gone wild! On *The Oprah Winfrey Show* one day, girls were sharing stories on how they participated in "Who looks best in a thong" contests. I personally want to ask what men are showing of themselves on TV, but we all know they're not showing anything!   I'm less concerned about the television shows and videos, and more concerned about the inner lack of confidence that likely exists in the participants. Ultimately, this results in a whole generation of youth chasing love with orgasms!

Unfortunately, it's not just youth, it's also moms and dads, a far cry from the past! You have some moms getting their freak on while their teenage boys chase the streets in the late hours of the night, finding nothing but trouble. Girls are performing sexually to fit in and feel freaky, so they can be "accepted." Guys not only want to feel freaky, but also powerful and free. While a man may pay a girl for her level of sexual activity, he surely won't marry the girl for it only! There may be a few exceptions, but usually these unions won't last. Trust, he's not in love with a stripper, he's in love with what the stripper does! He cares less about you and more about how you shake it, girl! He may pay you, but you'll never have all of him. You'll have to get what you can when you can. Are you really satisfied with this…running in the love chase marathon? Just because you have sex with him/her doesn't guarantee love in return. So, if love is what you're after, you can't win it that way. And, if you're using your body for anything less than love, you're selling yourself short. Even the best get caught up, including me. In high school, I danced my butt off and choreographed dance routines at parties and pep rallies! But, while I shook my booty, I didn't leave my brain empty. I kept things in perspective. There are plenty of ways to make money. It may not be the largest amount in the shortest time. It may not be the easiest to obtain. But, greediness leads to guilt! And how you obtained the money will eventually give you guilt, as well.

As with love, this isn't 100 percent. I met a 30-year-old medical student in Chicago and asked him what he was looking for in a woman. His first response was, "I just want to be happy." Then he added, "When I find a girl who gives spectacular good oral sex, I'm putting a ring on her finger quickly. For real!" I thought, "Wow, how stupid and simple is that!" He had to be ridiculous to marry someone for a single criterion like that! But in his case, good sex defines love. What works for you, works for you. Although, know that in most cases it's this type of love that won't last! And it's this type of love that has girls practicing the act over and over again, without success.

Love requires work. I went through one very long year of a "love" scandal. How did I allow him to convince me that I was as he said, "the manifestation of his prayer"? He prayed for "this and that," and supposedly I was the "this and that" and the one he should marry. The funny thing is, I did not start out praying for him. Notice, I said start out! Many women start praying for a particular man after just the first date and then tell the man that she's the one God has for him. A big no-no! For me, after falling for his words, I found myself asking God for him. I like to think I was covering myself at the time by also praying, "If it is your will, Lord." Neither of us did any work, just prayed. Thank God He doesn't always give us what we think we want. For real, we can pray ourselves into a hot mess! You can mistakenly ask God to give you hurt. Be careful what you pray for. I thank God His will was greater than my want. Yet, prayer without work is in vain! Love is not quick and easy. You're going to have to work, in order for it to work. My mother always tells me to guard my heart. It can be easy to fall in love. I've seen people who get serious about a man after just a few dates, apply pressure for commitment after sex, and act as though patience is just a word. Is a man to love you because you lay down with him in bed? Is a woman to love you because you took her shopping? Where is the work? Keep love in perspective. Study on this thought, it's not going to just happen.

Love has no guarantee. So you've put the work in to obtain love. You've discovered your purpose and nourished the love you have for someone by spending quality time and giving of yourself. You've also made sacrifices trying to prove your love to your mate. Yet, all of that seems not enough to him/her and the person decides to move on. Herein lays the risk involved in loving someone. While you work hard to receive love from the person, you can't make him/her love you in return, by no means. One of my male friends told me during my difficult first earthly love-like lust, "When a man wants to go, you can't make him stay." If the person stays with you, it's not necessarily to be with or marry you. It could be to keep getting some of the benefits that come with communicating with you, like sex with no strings attached. Some women think that by having sex, the relationship will move a step further. Not necessarily. Some women think that by getting pregnant, the man will marry her. Not necessarily. Pregnancy does not produce love, but it always produces a child, who has the right to be born knowing, not guessing, who his/her father is. Women should stop spoiling men with sex without commitment, if commitment is what she indeed wants. Dating someone doesn't come with a promise of commitment. Let your desires be known to the person early on. Hold true to what you want or you'll end up painfully hurt, led into deception and into the love chase game with no winner. Set a standard!

God searches the heart. The heart is deceitful above all things.
Jeremiah 17:9,10.KJV

Love hurts. Ooh wee does it hurt when it's gone bad! When love is good, it's good. But when it's bad, it's really bad! I mean, really! Everyone classifies love differently, resulting in broad definitions. Love that persists despite hurt is commonly described as real love, deep love, unconditional love, hard-core love, and even down-for-whatever love. Unless you're married and/or stayed with your first love, you've been hurt, whether you're a man or woman. But, hurting is not a revelation or manifestation of love. Meaning, just because you're hurt when the relationship ends doesn't prove that love ever existed! I know I'm not the only one who has once said, "I feel hurt. Wow, I must have really loved him." Wrong! It hurt that he disrespected and disregarded me, which did not equate to love! To many, the

110

thought of love is an excuse to accept abuse. What is it about this hurting love that many of us cannot separate from? There are so many signs and red flags that we disregard. Think about it, why do we ignore the "do not trespass" signs? Well, our hopefulness, which is mixed with nosiness, causes us to want to know what's back there. We think, "Maybe there *is* something good in this relationship." Those bright yellow lights telling us to "proceed with caution," why do we race through those? Instead of slowing down, we speed up because we're determined to get to the other side and really check this relationship out, again and again. We turn right and go the long way around the red stoplights that boldly say, "This is a no go! Ding! Ding! Ding"! Why? Because we believe we will find a way to make this relationship work. We are so very wrong! Just as we obey the traffic laws of actual red stoplights and yellow caution lights, so too are we not to proceed forward after realizing those bold flashy lights in our bad relationships.

If you have to search hard for it, it's not for you! We can mistakenly fall in love when we ignore the signs. We can force love on us, and hurt in the end, when we ignore the signs. The love in the short run feels good. But in the long term, it turns painful. We've all been there; when you love someone and feel as though you're getting so close to the person, and BOOM, he/she withdraws and rejects you. You try to deduce a reason, as he /she may have left you clueless, but you just can't figure it out. The person may even have ended things harshly and cruelly, even after things appeared to be going along well. So as a result, you second guess and blame yourself. Honey, the issue may not be you at all! Even without answers, you have to accept the rejection. I got over my hurt with the help of my mom and two friends, named earlier in this chapter, and gospel singer Kirk Franklin's "Hero" album. My spirits were up and down and intermingled with constant prayer and frequent calls to family and friends. I realized that for most of the encounter, I had placed God second, and that man first. The Word of God clearly says for us to have no other god before him and that he is a jealous God. He is the only being who is allowed to be jealous, and that, God definitely does! Considered usually quite spiritual, I felt guilty because of my response to this man and needed forgiveness.

The experience allowed me to see how sinners can be scared of walking into a church, thinking they don't fit in. At the time, I was tempted into believing that the church was for "clean" people and I had been wrong in letting God take the backseat. One day during that time, I went to church and sat outside in the parking lot in my SUV praying and listening to Franklin's album. Thank God for His omnipotence, as the spirit moved me with peace and understanding right where I sat. Even though the guy in this relationship showed me his hurtful behavior early on, I kept ignoring the signs and he stayed hurtful and insulting until the end. Despite that, it was difficult to let go. Then when it was over, this man attempted to cast blame on me. I remembered he told me something about himself in the beginning. In his own words, he described himself: "I can be a bastard!" Yes, he gave me not a hint, but a direct characterization of himself, a "red light," which I ignored. Usually, when you go through a red light, the police give you a ticket. Well, I went through a bold and bright "red light" and really needed to have gone to jail, not just get a ticket for that oops!

Your attempts to make something thrive that's not meant to be, will only work for a period of time. Nonetheless, prayer helped me see his wrong and my mistakes. I thank God for protecting me while I was walking blind and before I got in too deep. If you're starting to develop strong feelings for someone, but your feelings are not yet too deep, check and review yourself and your feelings. Make sure you're not following the interests and desires of the flesh. Take notice if you have ignored any wrongdoings by that person. Take notice if you have gone overboard. For some reason, I thought I would get love right the first time, but I didn't. Be careful not to make your desire to love be wrongfully relatable to the person you're dating who you know is treating you badly. Beware of the red flags and take heed to them early. When you do this, the hurtful feeling won't last as long!

Among whom also we all had our conversation in times past in the lusts of our flesh, fulfilling the desires of the flesh and of the mind; and were by nature the children of wrath, even as others.
Ephesians 2:3.KJV

Everyone is hurt at some point. So stop thinking you're alone in this. Others have gotten over the hurt and therefore you will overcome, as well. This scripture tells us that we've all been children of wrath by nature and there is a spirit of disobedience that exists in nature. We must fight this spirit. When you realize it's over, but you still want to see him/her, wanting to go to their home uninvited to prove your love, resist the temptation. I've been there. Even worse, I remember a patient while living in New Jersey who attempted suicide because her boyfriend of two years got another girl pregnant. A beautiful young lady sadly ready to give up her life. I remember another girl who damaged a man's car when he cheated on her. Also a beautiful lady, this one, ready to go to jail. We've all been there, wanting to revenge or hurt ourselves because we feel we can't go on. But you can! The ache is temporary and not worth the finalities of jail or death. Someone *may* send you a letter when you're in jail. Another *may* cry at your funeral. But no one is going to feel sorry for you, except for a quick moment. How do you get over the guilt after you realize you went overboard? First, don't go overboard. But if you do, read the above verse and the few following it. Learn and don't repeat!

It's hard to start over, as you may not know how. But, God can show himself most mighty when you're at your lowest point. When you're in pain, think of something God has blessed you with that you didn't think you'd get. Think of something he's already brought you through. If you think he hasn't done anything for you, at least he woke you up this morning. And yes, you can live another day! If you ask God to remove someone who you're finding may not be for you, be willing to accept it. Another friend helped me remember once, "Count the loss a blessing!" Believe that whatever good times you had with this person whom you thought would be your life partner, will be even better, no best, with the real love God has for you! To toot my own horn, I know my worth and you too, have to believe the right love for yourself. You will get through the love. You will love again! And you'll laugh at the past and ask yourself, "Why on earth did I try so hard to make that mess, yes mess, work? What was I thinking?" And the next time, if you stay in prayer, it will be that too-good-to-be-true, old school love!

Earthly love is not perfect! You may look at other couples and think, "Oh, they really have it going on." But really, you don't know what's going on inside their house. They may sleep in different rooms for all you know. I love the love that Jada and Will Smith represent! Yet, I know, as they have said, it's a natural love that still requires work. So don't look for a perfect love, you won't find it outside of God. No one is going to meet every quality on your list. 100 percent doesn't exist. Some believe love doesn't exist prior to marriage. I'm not sure about that one. But what I am sure of is that you shouldn't marry thinking a *perfect* love will abound during the marriage, as that marriage sadly becomes a partnership rather than a union!

Love begins with self! There is no guarantee you'll find that special earthly type of love. But don't put off love entirely. Begin with yourself. I don't mean decorating and redecorating yourself so you'll be loved in the *eyes* of someone else. You can be married and think you're in love and still be alone. Yes, many married couples are single at heart! Rather, start loving yourself by getting to know you, what you like to do and enjoy doing it by yourself. We've all heard, "If you don't love yourself, how do you expect someone else to love you?" If you don't like your hair, your nose, or other body parts, you'll inevitably point that out to your partner. Soon, that person will also not like your hair, nose, or other body part, as well as, you! My granddad used to say, "You came into this world by yourself, and you will leave this world by yourself." So, it seems that by yourself is where you should get comfortable being, right? Right! If in the end, if the earthly love experience is not for you, you still have yourself, baby! And that's more to lean on than the fake stuff!

Love happens again! You may not get love right the first time, or the second. I knew a man who thought every woman who came into his life was potentially his wife. This isn't so and if you think like him, you're bound for confusion! Everyone you meet is not spouse potential, and may not even be dating material. Love is a blessing. Some of us don't know what do to with blessings, be it a new job, money, or love. Some don't know how to keep a blessing from going to your head, or consuming you, making you go absolutely crazy! When you finally get the real love, how are you going to act? Will you have learned from the past and keep God the center, or will that person become your all and the reason why you live? Will you forget about you? Will you allow them to say and do anything just so you can be seen as having someone?

Can you stand to be blessed by an earthly love? Only you can answer that. If you didn't get it right the first time, you now know how to get through it and, if you so desire, love again. Next time, don't get lost in the process. Let's keep love in perspective and then we ultimately win.

THROUGH
THE ABUSE

Long after your physical scars, the black eyes, the cuts, the bruises, and possibly even the STDs have healed, the emotional scars still exist. These emotional scars will indeed survive, months and even years later, until an avenue towards recovery and newness is achieved. How long it takes for you to reach healing of the emotional scars of physical, domestic, and/or sexual abuse depends entirely upon you. Hopefully, you reach the point, as I did, where you are tired and fed up of wanting to believe in someone who claims to love you. And through your transition of feeling hurt, to acquiring newly developed anger, you find it easier to let go.

Power, to many, means dominion over people. When you can make someone directly or indirectly do what you say, that is power. A powerful person has respect, wealth, and acquires easy access to a variety of things. Some people know how to gain and use power in the appropriate way, while others misuse it, likely after obtaining it only by demeaning another. It's always interesting how those who feel less of themselves hit a slam dunk in finding someone who in turn, makes them feel like "somebody." It's way too common a situation that Sally married

Bill because his family is wealthy and she doesn't have to worry financially. Yet, what Sally should know is that Bill married her because she is easy to control, and he can exert power over her. There is this 180-degree turn in a weak person's ego that often comes through the degradation of another. Though they won't admit to it, they really believe, "I'm gonna make you feel little so I can feel like a king/queen!"

In high school, we called those people bullies. In love relationships, some excuse it by calling it actions of love. Yet, when a "loved one" knocks you up against a wall, chokes you, or takes advantage of your body, this does not signify truly loving you. No matter how much you want it to be true, Bill doesn't hit Sally to demonstrate loving her. In the process of abusing, he is able to feel better about himself while simultaneously relieving stress. It is the act that makes abusers love themselves, at least for that controlling moment. This is because of course, after the act, many abusers are so apologetic, as they are out of that violent mindset and may regret what physical hurt they caused. Others fail to see the hurt they caused, even when looking right at the black eye they created. So, there appears to be a quiet, peaceful time of variable duration until the need arises again to feel loved and powerful by hurting and belittling others. Even with the brief apologetic moment, there's no denying that the action has been done. There should be no erasing. I don't know who first formed this statement, but it's true, "Sorry is only good until the next time sorry has to be stated." When 1 in 4 women in a lifetime experience abuse; when an average 18 days per year will be missed at work because of the effects of abuse; and when an alarming 90 percent of women have problems at work, it's time to take a stand! You have to choose to live a life where "I'm sorry" and "I promise never to do it again" isn't all that you hear!

In speaking and hearing of married individuals and the pattern of love and abuse they sometimes find themselves in after the wedding, it's interesting how many of them mention having doubt about the person before the vows were stated. Abuse in this chapter, isn't always meant as physical or sexual, as there are many forms of abuse. It could also manifest as emotional, including causing mental challenges/games and confusion in relationships, persistent ignoring, withholding sex for selfish reasons, repetitive lying, and manipulative tactics. I will attempt to be specific as there is not a general healing mechanism for all types of abuse. Quite often, it's more common to be in a relationship where emotional abuse is the dominating or only form of abuse, and is often ignored, written off, and accepted as normal.

Many men get caught up with the tricks of some single, die-hard-wanna-be married-women, believing that the ease of the relationship prior to the wedding day exists after the honeymoon. I couldn't help but laugh when someone I know told me his relationship was going so smoothly, easy, and without any effort that he just knew that particular lady was the one and their love would be that way always. Anything that's natural with two very different people joining together is not that easy, and you have to wonder if someone is withholding something in order to make it easy. Specifically, this is emotional abuse, manifested as manipulation. She's showing him happy, happy, happy, until one day, BOOM, he's forced to ask himself, "Where did that drama come from?" Nothing good is gotten easily! Another man ignored signs of an overly powerful, selfish fiancé and married her anyway, only to now be expressively miserable. I can only shake my head from side to side, as the same complaints he had after the vows were the exact ones he mentioned and ignored before the marriage.

Of course, I've come in contact with many females who are married or in relationships where they too, ignored the signs of actual or impending physical and emotional abuse. We should think about this. If your husband cheated before you were married, now that you're married he will likely still cheat, as little change is made in a single wedding day. Even more so and contrarily, some women fall into the emotional traps of the I-forever-want-to-be-a-bachelor-man. For some reason, men have been led to believe that a couple of dinner dates equals a homerun in the bedroom, while not necessarily desiring to form a meaningful relationship. Even though you know you want more, you are now caught up in a cycle of sex only, wearing yourself out trying to convince him to want more from you. You might have even expressed to the man that you want more, but he will still attempt to give little to you and get much from you to keep you around, just before moving on to finding the next candidate.

We can become so caught up in wanting to be loved by that "special" person that we excuse the obvious. Excusing the obvious leads us directly into a trap when we know we need to let go. But by that time we have accepted the mess for so long we think it becomes worthwhile to continue and worthless to let go. Not true! Emotional abuse can be deceitfully good, as it conceals and suppresses the truth. When the truth finally manifests, it's at a point when you're not ready and when it has become too hard to let go.

It's good to be optimistic, but don't be anyone's fool! It's OK to give it a second chance, but when this second chance turns into thirds and fourths and fifths, you, I'm sorry, are tripping! Speaking to someone at the time of my abuse who physically abused a woman himself, helped show me the light! He said, "If he did it once, trust he'll do it again." Granted, change can come. But only with time and some sincere recognition and prayer. I knew the man I dated did not yet have these things. Setting a standard in relationships helps, but standing by those standards, although hard at times due to flesh, is what defines you and brings you closer to yourself, ultimately closer to finding true love. One of my mentors in emergency medicine told me, "Jeris, if you're presented with a patient, and if you *think* about ordering a test, you must order it, no second-guessing." Unfortunately, medical malpractice attorneys have helped increase the cost of ordering these tests, as even if we *feel* there may be a normal result, we *thought* about ordering it, and so the lawyers will *think* about suing us if we don't follow through with the thought. With abusive relationships, if we think about leaving, we should seriously consider it; you're welcome to be optimistic and try, try, try. But, if you don't *think*, rather you *know* you should leave, honey, you better make a dash for it fast! I know this is easier said than done. Trust, I know! But positioning is the key to advancement, not only in career goals, but also in abusive relationships.

When it comes to physical abuse, it's funny how the person doing the abusing, doesn't necessarily think it is abuse. They often have another definition of it. Commonly it's, "I raped her because I thought she wanted it." Or, "I raped her because when she said no, it sounded like a yes-no." Even, in my case while I was telling the man to hit the road his excuse was, "I choked you in order to relax you." And, "I choked you over and over, but I didn't leave any marks or hit you." They all sum up with, "I didn't *mean* to hurt you, even though I did." This can lead to another family situation I've seen firsthand in the ER, "I shot my pregnant girlfriend, but I only wanted to shut her up from our argument, not kill her." How brain receptors can cause people to rationalize bad behavior is a whole different subject. For now, just knowing that someone can in fact, rationalize bad behavior should be enough for you to make a dash for it. But often, it is not. This is because the abuser makes you feel as though you caused it, brought it on yourself, and you deserved it. They, in many cases, successfully make you feel that *you* need to change, get with *their* program so that *it* won't happen again. And so the cycle begins of you trying to figure out what it was that *you* did wrong, so that person won't abuse you again. First mistake!

No one deserves to be abused. I hate to bring up a double standard, but if a woman slaps a man most people, including strong men, agree that the man is not to place hands on that woman in return. No one does anything that warrants a man putting his hands on a woman inappropriately, versus him walking away. That woman, unless she is a body builder, will never be able to equal a man's strength. What women fail to see, is that person is simply violent, disrespectful, selfish, and unless you just like getting kicked around, he's not the one for you! For me, it took a few slam downs and three chokes in one night for me to make a dash for it. There's a split second during an abusive act, where you can decide to respond negatively or positively. In my situation, it could very well have had a bad ending. If I had not decided to run out of my apartment, dressed in what I had on, barefoot in a black satin robe, it could very likely have had a different ending. If he doesn't leave, you leave. Yes, I loved the man. But, I loved myself more not to give him another opportunity to abuse me, despite his infinite apologies and excuses. He could not buy me with all his riches. This, plus the fact I had been told so many lies and played into his demands and rollercoaster games of love long enough that I could handle no more.

Your body is a temple and any man who cares for you should value the temple, too. We need to recognize when we have been given a way out! Were there signs before the police had to be called? Yes, but I tried, tried, tried. Were there break-ups and make-ups? Yes, because I desired to be with someone and was deceived into believing that someone was him, until I figured enough excuses for this man had been made already. Ask yourself, "Is it worth all of this?" And hopefully you can answer, "No."

Positioning is everything! In business school, we learn this as one of the four P's. Goal seekers should in any scenario ask themselves, "How am I going to position myself for success?" Positioning makes it easier for you to say, "It's NOT worth all of this! Being with this person is NOT mandatory for me to be happy." If you base your life on that other person, it is harder to let go. If you depend solely on that person, your dash away is difficult to take. If along the way, you have given yourself up, given up on your career, and given all your emotions to that other person, you have set yourself up in a trap. You have to build yourself up, make your own way, so no matter how much money that person has or even how good their sex is, you don't need to rely on them. Otherwise, you're stuck baby, and choosing to leave means you have to start all over, not only in love, but in your own career and finances; a tough road to go down. It's one thing to start over, but it's a whole different task to find yourself again! The bad relationship may take away your pride, yet hopefully temporarily. But, don't let the relationship get you off track with your own goals and cause you to lose yourself. Having your own life, separate from theirs, provides you with a way out if it fails.

I looked at myself and could firmly say, "I don't need him and I don't need his money." Some people stay tied in an abusive relationship, be it emotional or physical, because they have made themselves need that person for something. Whether it's for money, sex, authority, or name, you have trained your mind to think that outside of that person, you cannot do better. When I think of a young lady I met, who continues to be the other woman to a "happily" married man despite his emotional abuse, again I can only shake my head side to side. She knows she should take a dash for it and leave him alone, but apparently this unemployed "happily" married man puts it down in the bedroom so good, she obviously feels she cannot find better. I met another female college-graduate-turned-stripper, who settled into a mansion with a wealthy man who offered her everything; everything at a cost of physical abuse. She stayed with him for a long time, until finally she saw the light. Yet, the person doing the abuse doesn't have to be sexually talented or wealthy. They may be broke, mean and ugly, and still have a hold on you because of your low self-esteem.

Many times, just the desire to be married can be self-induced emotional abuse and lead you into remaining with a man/woman just for love. Ultimately, you settle in choosing to be with that person and often let your career goals go bye-bye. Yes, relationships are give and take. Yes, you should give part of yourself in the process of joining with another. But when you find yourself giving all of yourself, and/or when anything your partner is giving is hurtful, honey it's time to make that dash and try again with someone else, if you feel the need to be with someone.

Positioning in relationships doesn't always mean self-financial stability. It is a mindset, as well. You need to be strong enough and confident enough to say, "Hit the road Jack, you mean me no decent good." My thoughts were, "I've dated more respectful men than this abusive guy! So, for my future, there's got to be better men than this trifling individual." Even now, without revealing who this man I dated was, I wish the best for him and pray for his well being. We both knew at the end of the relationship that the period was a growing time for us individually. In your next relationship, be firm to position yourself not for weakness, but for solo-greatness. You came out of your mother's womb solo, which means despite joining with someone in partnership, you still are an individual with an individual purpose.

The breakaway can be harder than the actual abuse. As soon as you think you're done with the physical abuse, the emotional aspect thrives. If it takes more to let go, which often it does, tell yourself, "There's got to be better!" When the person tries to win you back with their "come-back" tales and tactics, tell yourself and the person again, "There's got to be better!" A lady hit the hammer dead on the nail when she said, "Every time I feel I'm able to move on, he makes me feel guilty with calls and messages like, 'Remember the good times. All couples have problems.'" Comments like those seek to make you think the relationship was the norm. Men can get it too, as women will say, "Let's stay together for the kids. If you leave me, you won't see your son (or daughter) again." When you hear things like this, you have to say to yourself, "Whatever! I'm still leaving as there's got to be better!" But the only way you can say that with confidence is if you've not only positioned yourself in a way that you can firmly say goodbye, but you've also taken time to meditate on a reality check. Otherwise, you are stuck and will quickly give in to the tactics, as though they are truth.

The necessity of a reality check is often not accomplished because of fear. No matter how bad your present situation or relationship is, you somehow think that reality checking is *worse*? I like to think of it this way. The longer you take to perform a reality check, the more in danger you are in your present situation, and the longer it takes for you, and maybe also your family, to be in peace. No matter how gloomy you think your future looks without that person, the reality check is what allows you to see a remote glance at some sort of breakthrough. If you can at least say, "What if I wasn't with this person," hopefully you can see that the "what if" alone, opens up possibilities. I'm concerned for women/men who believe the lie when a man/woman tells them, "You can't do better without me. No one else will want you." I didn't realize how common this was until I spoke with more and more women. Many of them get to the reality checkpoint and start to ask questions, but they believe in the wrong possibility. Asking questions like, "What if I can't live without him/her?" My response, "Well, if you couldn't live without him, yal would've been Siamese twins, joined at the hip or somewhere." Or they wonder, "What if I can't find anyone better than him/her?" Think about this. If you're meant to spend the rest of your life with someone that person will come into your life at the appropriate time. Others ask, "What if he/she comes back to hurt me if I leave?" That's a scare tactic that's bound to convince you into bondage if you believe it. Instead, you should be wondering what if he/she hurts you again if you stay with him/her?

Even some say, "But we were together for years and built a 'life' together." My reply, "If you wake up tomorrow, your future life is ahead of you." Others cry, "But the people who doubted us will be made right!" So what! They were right! No one's counting but you. They'll still be right when you're dead or in jail! You may say, "But what if I can't face people. They're so used to seeing us together." Well, how did you face them with the black eye? Or how did you face them believing in the lie that everything was OK in the relationship? Then, you had to fake it. At least now, you can be real! Lastly, a common question is, "What if I have to raise my kids alone?" Hey, it isn't the ideal situation, but plenty of individuals have simultaneously been both the mother and the father, and successful at it. Haven't you seen any of the real-life stories on the *The Oprah Winfrey Show*?

These "what if" questions go on and on, racing through the brain. The good thing is, asking them opens up a 50-50 chance of success. Without asking them, there's a 100 percent chance of failure! Recognize that you have a choice. Reality-check yourself and see that a better possibility is out there, even if the better is being without a man/woman, even if the better is being broke for awhile, even if the better is being a single parent, even if the better is being stalked for awhile, or even if the better is learning to make your own decisions. The infamous saying is, "I can do bad all by myself." Believe it! Seriously, if you feel you would suffer if alone, at least you'd be suffering in peace! Suffer in peace!

Getting through the abuse is surely not easy. Positioning is hard, as it does require quite a bit of wits and pre-planning. And yes, reality checking is intense, as it requires quite a bit of guts and risk-taking. But, regrouping? Wow, that's even more of a biggy! So, you've finally decided to go with the positive end of the "what if" questions and now you have to deal with the "consequences" of choosing the right way. I know, you're thinking that all things are supposed to be positive now that you've let go, right? So why am I calling it consequences? This is because you have dealt in that bad situation long enough, likely made plenty of wrong decisions in the process, and now that you wanna get back on track, the consequences of your past wrong decisions are what you now have to face. Statistics show that more women are the recipients of physical abuse, so for simplicity, I will refer to this fact.

One example of "consequences" is a woman who allows a man to beat her, lets her mind become emotionally screwed up so she can't work, and thus loses her job. That happened to me! Now the consequence is, she's lost her job and has to search for a new one. Another example is when a woman has allowed a man to control her and everything about her, resulting in losing friends and a sense of self. The consequence is, she has to find new friends and revisit who she is. While consequences require a little work to get through, the good thing is they are temporary. Although easily confusing, it shouldn't be considered a punishment or jail sentence, which can take a longer period of time to push through. Yet, consequences really only take less time to overcome when you recognize them early and are willing to work to get beyond them.

Regrouping begins with forgiving yourself and moves on to culminate in relearning yourself. I'm sure we can all think of a situation we regret. For me, before I forgave myself for a particular decision, it ate me up whenever I thought about it. I kept asking myself, without ever reaching an answer right away, "What was I thinking?!" I know my mom got tired of me asking the same question! And if you have no regrets then somehow you're a rare perfect one, a walking Jesus of some sort, and I'd sure like "to touch the hem of *your* garment" and have some of that perfection brush off on me. I often wondered why it is sometimes harder to forgive ourselves for some things. I mean we live with ourselves, right? So, it should just seem easier that we be able to forgive ourselves. I haven't completely figured that one out yet. But I'm leading to postulate that it has a little to do with our ego, possibly thinking we were just too great of a person to commit that bad decision, thus making it even harder for us to swallow.

The simplest way to begin the process of forgiving yourself is to recognize that we all make mistakes. I remember that was my mom's advice during my abusive situation. She really had nothing else to say, as it was that simple. Now, I see that was all that needed to be said. I made a mistake in selection. We all mess up at some point. Yes, you too, if not already, will make a wrong decision if you live long enough. Just pray your mess-up doesn't land you in jail or in a casket before your time. It was this phrase which helped me realize I needed to forgive myself for even being in that situation, giving it chance after chance. I've heard a lot and even in the emergency room, I've seen a lot. Whatever your case, be it forgiving yourself for that extra drink, knowing you're way past your limit, forgiving yourself for the unprotected sex, forgiving yourself for accepting the excuses, or forgiving yourself for choosing a path you knew would lead to danger, you, too made a mistake. The mistake may be life-altering, but it's NOT life-determining.

Once you've forgiven you, it's time to relearn. Relearn what it means to truly give love. Relearn what it means to truly receive love. Relearn what it means to reach your own goals, desires, and purposes. Relearn what it means to sacrifice and reap benefits, not harsh name-callings and manipulations. Relearn how it feels to have inner peace. Relearn what it means to have self-control. Relearn what it means to make your own decisions. Relearn what it means to answer to you. Relearn what it means to be you, to please you. How do you begin to do this? I'm not a personal user of this action, but many people like journal writing, keeping a log of your daily events. At least, when you take time to look over it, you can see with your own eyes a cycle of negativity, which you can study and correct. Self-help books are great, too. Knowledge is definitely key. Seeking insight and wisdom from those who've dedicated years to observation and behavioral therapy can go a long way. Group therapy, although may appear awkward to some, provides a direct means to see others in similar situations like yourself. It opens a door for new friendships and can create partnerships in the battle to get through the abuse. I haven't done this, and people commonly laugh about this path, but seeking individual counseling or a shrink at least provides a way for you to talk things out. Look into professional treatment if indeed your situation is serious or debilitating.

Surrounding yourself with positive people, commonly found at church gatherings, is another way to learn new things. Yet, expanding on this a bit further, recognize that there does exist feelings of inadequacy and filthiness, experienced by some, which may prevent you from entering a church. Despite your feelings of worthlessness, despite your opinions that everyone in the church is judgmental, there is an open door, which offers you the same path to spiritual greatness as the "best of people." Know that the "best of people" were surely not always that way. As Pastor Donnie McClurkin sings in a popular song, "A saint is just a sinner who fell down and got up." Although it may seem to some like a foreign language, picking up the Bible can provide a wealth of wisdom, and with prayer, opens up a direct path for God to speak to you. Anything that's happening now has happened in the past. If you're tired of looking at the way the world does things nowadays, reading the Bible and creating your own definition of life and living is a perfect way to start.

A person can have it all going well, and yet someone else, who likely feels little, can make that person feel as though they too, belong at the bottom of a pole. It's worth remembering that you had a life before someone else entered it. True, in some cases, your life might not have been worth a toot. But, you had a life.

Recognize this last step in getting through the abuse, re-living. You once had a purpose before you met that person. Whether you knew what the purpose(s) was, is a different entity, but you had one. It's likely that in the midst of your trying to be another person's everything, you lost your self, *your* life. Re-live! Oftentimes, you fail to see a distraction, even though it's not only "staring you in the face," but beating you in the face, as well. Getting caught up in the excuses thereafter, creates a tunnel, depth, and windmill of confusion. At some point, asking yourself, "How did I get here," opens the path toward recognizing, regaining, and re-living your life. Say, "No" to the drama, and "Yes" to you! Living dangerously is not the way you have to live. So re-live!

When I overcame my physical abuse and decided to make a dash for it, I initially found myself sharing the experience with others, as though I was a victim. Then one day I thought, "Victim is such a negative word. I'm not in that negative situation anymore. I survived that!" Truly, you're only a victim as long as you stay in that situation. When you're strong enough to let go, you become a survivor. As long as you're in that situation, you're considered to be a victim. But it sounds so much better to describe yourself as a "survivor," doesn't it? Well, this can only happen if or when you decide to push through the abuse. So "knock it out" of your life figuratively, that is. Seriously, it's time to roll; it's safer to make that dash. It's going to be great to start over, and don't look back now, "ya hear"?

Chapter Ten

THROUGH
THE STORM

> "Fear not those things which God has sent
> though troublesome they may seem. For he knows best
> what must be done to help you reach your dream."
> –Author Unknown

Although the world is full of suffering, it is also full of overcoming it. There's nothing dimmer than the day *after* a storm. The actual storm, yes, it is a difficult picture to look at. But that morning *after*, when you note the leftover damage, *that* is the tough cookie to swallow, especially when at times, you didn't know you would even make it out of the storm!

I used to think about how lucky some folks are to go through life seeking their goals or whatever, succeeding without difficulty. Going through medical school, hearing of students who had parents who paid cash for college and graduate training, or purchased homes for their kids so they would simultaneously be investing while studying, definitely made my mouth drop in awe. There were even students who had extensive stock portfolios, one person right after graduating from high school! All this would leave me wondering, "Wow, it must be nice to have it easy! No worries." We all know those people or have seen them on

129

television. They seemingly have it all going for them, focus from the start, and money. Their path is laid out and straightforward without any ragged edges. Now, I see those people as boring and look at them with hesitation as though, "If you had to go through the same hard things others face, you wouldn't make it even halfway." I'm not knocking on the "very fortunate," as I want my children to have it made, going through much less than their parents, but still going through some sort of storm. After all, there's a blessing in the storm. It isn't meant to kill you, but to produce something greater in you.

Every experience is a potential resource. Yes, every experience. When the bad news hits you so hard that you feel as though you might faint, in that very experience, there is a "potential" gain, a blessing. It may look very hopeless at first. You could very well be on the verge of losing it all, but if you march on, even after you lose all, there is a "potential" for gain. Having faith in this "potential" is one thing that can get you through the storm. When the amount of medical school loans were starting to mount up and I had to move out of my apartment, there were no other feelings but discouragement and fear that came about me. It's funny how trying to do something right in life is often accompanied by interferences of wrong and negative things. Despite the fear, many open doors were provided to me. Planning hospital rotations my last two years around those that provided housing was indeed a major plan. Yet, it was not as easy as you might think.

Packing up every month, loading and unloading in every dormitory-style room, and traveling long distances from Columbus, Ohio, to Buffalo, New York, to Newark, New Jersey, to Bethlehem, Pennsylvania, to Atlanta, Georgia, was not thought to be a complete vacation, as going to all those places would seem! Initially, my thoughts were that each move was a different phase of a storm. I had the wind, the forceful rain, and roaring thunder. At one point, I chose to take different perspectives—it was driving through the Poconos many times, deciding to note their beauty; it was stopping to feel the mist and energy of Niagara Falls that I found amazingly relaxing; and it was pulling over alongside a highway during an actual rainy storm, only to see a deer walk straight up next to my car—that helped me see God taking me to new experiences and heights. I initially thought of all that moving around as unbearable, but learned to appreciate the beauty in seeing all that the different states had to offer. Hey, after all that moving, there are only a few states left in the U.S.A. I have not visited! So, one of the first things that can help us get through storms, is realizing that it isn't always as bad as it seems.

While riding up to Washington, D.C. for my Sorority initiation, my mom met a woman who said it best, "Don't look at the situation. Look at the hands who hold the situation." That stormy situation may look so bleak and be so depressing. But first try looking at it under a different light. When we go to light a dark room, it isn't just one kind of light bulb we can use to get the sort of lighting we want. There are all sorts of watts! If 40-watt isn't bright enough, we can increase it to 60-watt. And if 60-watt is still too dim, we can think of using 100-watt. The point is, there really is no limit as to how far we can go in determining how much, or little, we will light a dark, dim room. The choice is ours. As such, when the rain starts pouring harder, don't say, "Man, I'm gonna get soaked out there today." Rather, turn it around positively and say, "Wow, that rain surely sounds good and relaxing hitting hard on the roof!" When the thunder roars, don't get scared. Instead, imagine the same sound as though the clouds are rumbling together in passionate beauty. When lightning strikes, think of it just as a firecracker or something spectacular lighting up a dark, black, cloudy night. Believe this while staying far from a tree, however!

Things aren't what they seem necessarily, but they are as *you see* them. How you see your dreary situation will determine the outcome. I heard it once said as, "You are what you think you are." So it doesn't start with the storm itself, but how you perceive the storm. Put in real perspective, being broke can be a blessing. Think of it as, "If I was never broke, how would I know what it's like to be rich?" Because when you become rich, you may not really appreciate it had you not been broke. You may run and avoid opening the bills now. But if you're working towards a goal, despite your current stormy situation, sooner or later you can request for automatic deduction to pay those same bills from one of your many checking accounts. When your guidance counselor tells you that the cost of education is high and you think you can't afford it, think positively. Change it around to say, "The cost may be high, but there is money out there and I will find it, borrow it, or apply for it until I get it!"

There's nothing that should be more inspiring than hearing of a homeless person turn millionaire, owning real estate and mortgage companies. What do you think drives them? What was it that you think got them through their storm? It wasn't money! Maybe it was their faith? Or perhaps it was their determination? Maybe it was their belief that a turn-a-round was bound? Or was it their confidence? Perhaps it was their friendliness that caused a wealthy person to see and invest in their goal? Whatever it was, it was definitely positivity, not money, initially.

> For which of you, intending to build a tower, sitteth not down first, and counteth the cost, whether he have sufficient to finish it."
> Luke 14:28.KJV

Oftentimes, we put the problem before the promise. It's easy to get sidetracked and distracted focusing on all the problems rather than remembering that you were promised. Even the Word of God says we are to live life and live it more abundantly. That's a promise! When you pray believing you will reach a particular goal that is a promise. We can be so caught up during the process and some of us give up with all the issues that we never make it to the promise. You let the storm rough you up so you even forget that you had been promised. While you ride through the storm, through the difficult time, through the discouraging event, be careful to remember that you're walking on something that is already guaranteed. Think of getting through an issue as having an established, positive end. This turns the focus away from the many problems we face en route to the end result. Don't misunderstand me, as the problems ultimately help make the end greater. Yet, so many people give up while going through so much. I must bring particular attention to the importance of keeping the focus on the promised end result.

There's no other place in the U.S.A. that I'd rather go through difficult times than in beautiful San Diego. Funny enough, no matter what bland situation I faced, every morning the sun was shining, the air was fresh, the city surroundings were clean, and the water was peaceful, creating an environmental covering of bad problems. There's definitely something to be said about residents in these areas, as well as states like Vermont and New Hampshire, and why statistics show they live longer than other residents living the "city lifestyle." One thing I realized, while living there and going through a storm, was not to put my struggle behind me without my due reward. I went out there with a dream of becoming the first physician in my family. No matter what, that was going to be the end result.

In the educational program, we were not allowed to work. So, naturally funds were tight. The second half of the year, however, I had no choice but to find some sort of part-time gig and decrease my participation in the program a bit. Once, during renovations and insect prophylaxis treatment, my apartment building managers offered to pay for a 2-night hotel stay versus giving discounted rent. I had passed the point where I could ask my folks for more money. Well, I could, but you can get tired of asking your family to continuously help you out. So, I decided to take the discounted rent. It was early in my arrival to San Diego and I did not really feel comfortable asking colleagues if I could cram at their place. So, I lived in my car for those days, parking it at the neighborhood Ralph's Grocery Store parking garage. Man, those days allowed me to get a firsthand grasp at what homeless people go through. Trying to find places to use the bathroom, wash up, and having people look at you like you're crazy as you try to be incognito in your car and sleep without needing to watch your back, were just some of the things I experienced. Thank God I had only to bear it two days and nights, but knowing that people in our country have to do this day in and day out is treacherous abandonment. Yet, despite their storms, some of the happiest and friendliest people are homeless. So, when the acceptance letter to medical school finally came in after all the dozens of rejection letters, I wept tears of joy the entire walk from my mailbox to my apartment!

You should realize that you are predestined. No matter what you have to go through in-between time, you will get there if you persevere. Think less about how much money you don't have or how many people tell you what you can't do. Remember that you are predestined. You may be rocked in the storm. However, prayer and God will help you rock steady. You may be displaced. But, the same off-trail that got you all "off track" can lead you to the same finish line.

Having been through a few storms and seeing how getting caught up can have you give up, I learned that though the problems make us stronger in the end, it truly can be hard to see the blessing while in the midst of the storm. At times, when I heard my mom or a pastor say, "There's a blessing in the storm," I would be one to definitely ask, "Oh yeah, where? Please tell me where cuz I don't see it!" Of course, my mom would say, "Wait, just wait. You'll see what I'm telling you." I found a scripture that's almost a perfect one to rely on in the midst of a stormy situation.

> Better is the end of a thing than the beginning thereof:
> and the patient in spirit is better than the proud in spirit.
> Ecclesiastes 7:8.KJV

When it's all said and done, it will be worth it in the end. When you get that management position you have been diligently working for, when you get the healing you have been praying and going to treatment for, when you get the wife you have been searching for, that end will be much greater than when you started. The process looks tedious, but the end result is better because of the route you had to take. Appreciate the process, which is special and unique to you. You might not value the new job if you did not have to go through so much to get hired. Hey, you may even be a better parent now that you had to undergo in vitro fertilization in order to have a child. Allow God to raise you to another level by going through the struggles. Rather than asking yourself what else or what time you would have gained had you not gone through something, ask yourself what you would have lost if you hadn't gone through it. Don't quicken your tribulation and don't add to your tribulation by worrying and taking matters in your own hands. Keep hope until the end is clear!

Most of us have heard of the story of Jesus sleeping in the midst of a tornado. He didn't worry, he didn't fret. Jesus simply said, "I'm going to bed." Today, we can ebonically rephrase that and say, "I ain't gonna lose no sleep!" It's something about being at ease in the middle of a catastrophe that is not only admirable, but respectful. The former New York City Mayor, Rudy Giuliani, demonstrated this best to the world in September 2001. He didn't get angry, he didn't get vengeful; he led a city peacefully to recovery, through a horrible and unexpected storm. Christians call that sort of peace, faith. Likewise, when you see the waves of problems hovering over you and you can still go to sleep, that's faith. When you've been told a bad diagnosis and you still believe in healing, that's faith. When I lost my residency position, I put my fighting gear on and went to sleep. Yet, I didn't even have to fight as two days later, the decision was reversed. I had faith. 2 Timothy, Chapter 2, Verse 3 says we "are to endure hardness as a good soldier." Soldiers put their war gear on and prepare for battle. Thankfully, not every battle is ours to fight and faith allows us to rest. Paul says in The Word, "I will look to the hills from which cometh my help." When you do that, you definitely won't lose any sleep!

We are troubled on every side, yet not distressed.
We are perplexed, but not in despair, persecuted but not destroyed.
2 Corinthians 4:8,9.KJV

In talking to people, some of us can misunderstand who is to suffer and go through problems. Many people believe that only bad people go through storms and that you must have done something really bad to be going through all the "drama"! I remember a lawyer in Chicago, who turned out to be trifling after taking me from pro bono (refusing my money), to charging me high fees when I would not have sex with him. His thoughts were that I must have made someone really upset after I mentioned my domestic abuse and job issues. It was funny how he could tell me that he has sex with another client, who had become his "homegirl" during the process of defending her in a child support case, to asking me for some bedroom love as well. And it was unethical for him to all of a sudden elicit "brand-new-ism" in charging me, after I passed on his sex offering. I told him that God lets the good and bad see the sunshine and he lets the rain pour on everyone. Truth is, all "blessings" don't come from God, as Satan keeps his people bling-blinging and in positions of impressionability, too. No matter how good you think you are, you are not exempt. As a matter of fact, as a child of God, seeking perfection and his grace, you are "instructed to suffer for Christ's sake." Shall Jesus bear the cross alone?

There is no other storm in history that exemplifies this than Hurricane Katrina in 2005. I am still amazed at how the government, national and Louisiana state, and insurance companies have apparently left those tax-paying victims and New Orleans city mayor to fight for themselves. The mayor shouldn't have to ask in 2007, "Where is the money?" Literally, that storm moved everyone in that area. No matter whether you were rich, poor, good, or bad, you were hit hard by the stormy, rising waters of Katrina. No matter how hard you prayed, you saw the damage. You might have even had money to fly out, but the damage was there for you to see when you returned. Of course, families asked, "Where's the blessing in that storm?" I honestly don't know. But, God does. Even if you think you've found the blessing, it may not necessarily be what you think it is. Understand that getting through the storm may take some time. However, I've realized that with every burden, grace grows stronger. With every affliction, I see Him move. With every trial, I witness a triumph. So, it may look unpromising. You might have lost everything. But, remember that after the loss, comes a gain. After the storm or the drought period, comes record-breaking great weather. Yes, the day after is even more depressing than the actual storm, as reality of the damage sets in. But, if you can hold on through the change, keep your motivation high despite what things look like, and not give up, you will ultimately see how God is a storm fixer, a way maker, a task breaker, a wind calmer, a burden bearer, and a load carrier.

Sometimes, as soon as you get through one storm, here comes another. You see yourself getting back on track, then oops, here comes another trial. I remember speaking to a patient who had been through one diagnosis, to another diagnosis, to another diagnosis. I was inspired by her strength in not letting it all get her down. My grandfather once said, "It's not the one who works and quits in the middle who succeeds, but the one who fights until the end." During my last year in medical school, there were a few storms I had to go through. I must say, as soon as I thought I was good to go, bam…another surprise. It's funny how I could rotate and move from hospital to hospital and everything was safe and peachy, only to arrive to my home state of Georgia and experience crime myself. I even rotated at an inner-city hospital in New Jersey, where another medical student was held up at gunpoint right outside our living quarters.

This all really took me in amazement! I swear, it was only a good twenty minutes of check-in after I parked my car in front of the dorm for a rotation at Grady Memorial Hospital in Atlanta, Georgia. I was parked directly in front of a parking garage that had a security guard on site, but I returned to find my back window busted and items stolen from my car. If someone would have had a camera to record my facial expression, with my mouth wide open and eyes wide open, for a very, very long time walking around and around my car in disbelief, it probably would have been a winning video for America's Home Videos! You would have thought I saw an alien or UFO! And to think, no one in the area knew or saw anything, even though it was 4:30 in the afternoon and people were going in and out of buildings.

That day, I really wanted to leave and forego the rotation, not caring that the act would have put me back for graduation. I was upset with that welcoming expression from my home state! I stayed, but to top it off, at the end of the rotation, it seemed that I wasn't going to make it out of Atlanta to my next rotation in Ohio after I got a severe case of food poisoning! I had ongoing symptoms even after large doses of medications and fluids, and the ER doctors wanted me admitted to the hospital! They gave me four or five liters of fluid, but I was still out of it! Even my old friend, a physician himself, had never seen a patient in so much symptomatic distress as I was in. But, I told those doctors, "No, I got to get out of here, this city, now! It's not doing me any good here. Just give me some more fluid and a few more minutes to try to get it together to walk and I'll be OK." Seriously!

If thou faint in the day of adversity, thy strength is small.
Proverbs 24:10.KJV

I would have been a little chump to run away after my car was broken in. Although I was heated after they stole my laptop, in the end, the insurance company reimbursed me. As for the timely food poisoning, there was nothing good that came out of that. But it was a distraction that could have hindered me if I had not fought through it. I've heard it said by some as, "Trials are stumbling blocks, not stopping stones." With each issue we face, although it can be difficult, we have to remember to stumble, not stop. Tell your problems as I told those doctors in Atlanta, "I'm getting out of here. I'm moving on!" Please don't take this literally, as there is nothing worse than a patient leaving against medical advice (AMA). I did not leave AMA, as they were able to feel comfortable discharging me after I assisted the doctors by asking them to quicken my treatment in order to cut the hospitalized time. And most of all, I'm a physician as they are, who knew my limits and what further to do in my treatment. Try seeing your problems as a chance to learn your strengths, as an opportunity for God to teach you how to hold up and stand up in a tragedy, calamity, or disappointment.

I refer to many scriptures in this book, but I am not a preacher. I am not perfect. I just learned early that there are two things that can help govern and guide us through life. One, is fearing God. When we do this, it sets up a sense of conviction that can help us do right, at least a majority of the time. Another, is believing in God's plan. As when we do this, we see that everything works in his plan. However, some negative results happen because we caused them. We cannot blame God for everything. One true preacher, Bishop Horace Smith, M.D., of Apostolic Faith Church in Chicago, Illinois, stated one Sunday, "You can't live by reasoning. God doesn't see facts. He's not to be understood, only to be revealed." Of course, I said, "Amen" to that! You may ask, "Why do I have to go through such a situation?" First, see if you caused it, if you made a mistake. Then, if not, if you truly believe you've been doing the best you can and everything right as much as possible, living righteously, treating people right, being faithful, praying consistently, then it's OK to ask, "Why, God, why?" However, be prepared that you may never get an answer, or at least not the answer you want. Worrying your brains out, trying to figure and reason the situation, creating risks for stress-induced stomach ulcers, is not worth it. You may not understand it, but you may see a revelation from God in time. One of the great Negro spirituals states it best, "We'll understand it better by and by. By and by."

> For I reckon that the sufferings of this present time are not worthy
> to be compared with the glory which shall be revealed in me.
> Romans 8:18.KJV

This is another absolute favorite scripture that can be meditated upon to get you through the storm. I don't quite remember which storm I was tackling when I came across this one in the Bible. But, I do remember feeling a sense of desperation in seeking God for answers and guidance, praying before directly opening my Bible to this scripture. The sense of relief that came over me after reading it just the first time, is totally indescribable. Reading that what I was going through could not even compare to the end glory just made me ecstatic! Seriously. It turned my worry straight into anticipation. I went from, "Man, what am I gonna do? How am I gonna make it?" To, "Wow, how fantastic the end is going to be! I cannot wait! Bring it on!" This scripture demonstrates that there are indeed sufferings we must go through, as though a price for a blessing. God's grace is free. But are blessings?

We know how free things are handled, right? Some people don't necessarily take care of free things. If we lose something we didn't pay for, we might not bother to even look for it! We think at times, "I didn't have to pay for it, so if I lose it, oh well." Or, "It didn't cost me anything, so it really doesn't matter what happens." These nonchalant feelings don't even exist when we've worked hard for something, or gone through something to gain a thing. When we pay for something, there is value, so it's harder to let go, to give up. Thoughts in this situation are, "I went through this and I struggled to do that? No way, I'm not letting go." It's interesting how paying for something adds worth. It becomes an investment. Likewise, there is a price for a blessing. You pay the price by going *through* the storm and it is the very same storm that should make it harder for you to give up!

The same way you think of paying for material things, think of equating going through struggles as paying for a blessing. Victory feels all the better after a war is actually fought and won. If the other team or opponent gives up or is a no-show, who cares if you won by default, you didn't have to fight! Common sentiments are, "So what! You didn't struggle for anything!" But when you go through the hurt, the pain, the disappointments, the struggle, the storm, that victory is immeasurable! Man, it feels great to actually fight and win! You worked hard, suffered long, and you did it! Moreover, you can never be able to do what God has for you to do, if you haven't been through anything. Do as Galatians tells us, "Be not weary in well doing, for in due season, you shall reap if you faint not."

Don't let the storm and the struggles move you, rather, you move through it. Truth is, there is no doubt that the storm will pass over! The sun will definitely rise again, but will you be happy and able to appreciate the rainbow? Or will you be down and out because you gave up when the wind and struggle got a little rough? The real question is not if you will get through the storm, but if you will be situated and prepared to handle the "afterstorm"? Will the storm take over you, or will you have successfully gone through it? Will you be less off or better off? It's up to you to rule the universe. When you see the waves encroaching, and when the stuff in your life seems to be turning upside down, you now know things to help you tackle the storm. Mother Nature may bring the storms, but you're the captain of the ship. So get ready to be rocked. But rock steady! Rock steady in faith, knowing that you were promised and the end will be greater than the beginning!

Chapter Eleven

THROUGH
THE ARRIVAL

▷ ► ▷ ► ► ► ►

We are always arriving. At least we should be. I believe we never reach a point of finality until we are dead. They say it's "not over until the fat lady sings." Why it isn't over until *somebody* sings and why that somebody has to be a fat lady, I don't know. But, she's not singing in my life, except at a funeral. I'm going to keep on climbing, keep on arriving until it's really, officially over. Likewise, while you have reached your goal, while you have succeeded through everything, you should attempt to reach even new and greater heights.

Before I glorify and celebrate those people who *know* they have arrived, let me first encourage those of you who are still striving, and struggling to reach your goal and make it just once in your life. There are at least six reasons why your arrival is delayed. One reason may be that you are seeking something for all the wrong reasons. There is little sincerity in the process. Second, you may be scared to be different. Third, you may place yourself first and God last. Remember, he wants to get the glory in giving you the blessing. Fourth, you may possess an attitude of being easily satisfied. God doesn't just want to bless you once. He wants you to live life abundantly. The fifth reason lies in an old book with modern thought

141

that I read back in college. This particular book is by T. D. Jakes of The Potter's House in Dallas, Texas, *Can You Stand To Be Blessed?* In reading this book, the title alone can have someone pondering, "What does he mean can I stand to be blessed? Of course I can!" Not necessarily so! Positioning yourself for a blessing was stressed earlier in this book. Truth is, God knows exactly what you would do if he blessed you. He knows if you will go crazy. He knows if you will overspend. He knows if you will think too highly of yourself. He knows if you will allow the blessing to rule you. He knows if you will place the blessing before God. When the blessing leads you into a path of negativity, you cannot stand to be blessed. So the fifth reason is that you may not know how to handle success. The sixth reason is that many people have not learned to enjoy the arrival before it actually takes place. You cannot put your joy, your happiness on hold until the arrival comes as then, you are living for the arrival. Live life now!

If you have yet to arrive at something, you should know that there is a difference between going through the motions and deciding to take an active stand, working hard to reach that goal. You should not just say you're not going to fail. You have to really believe it, let the thought govern your every move, confidently realizing that failure is not an option. I'll say again what I said earlier, that many of us are on the verge of a blessing and thus, on the verge of an arrival.

Some of us don't make it to the arrival because we lack support. For example, you may believe there is no reason for you to do well on your report card because there's no one to look at it, there's no one to help you with your homework, and there's no one with whom to celebrate your successes. You have to learn to believe that as commonly stated these days, "You are a force to be reckoned with." If people are not in your corner, you must believe that they are the ones standing on the wrong side of the street. Succeed for yourself. You may not have a crowd of folks saluting you. You may not have anyone who cares that you do well on your report card. But, congratulate yourself, throw your own party and be sure to make a toast to yourself!

My grandfather used to say, "We all come to the Red Sea of life." He would go on to add that we all come to a place where we are forced to stop. You may be well on your way to a successful arrival, but you will reach a stopping point where the waves and winds are so harsh and the problems so many. Your mistake may even be the cause of the uproar, but either way at this deadlock, you decide to give in and turn around, or you believe by faith that you will walk on. When you decide to walk on, and walk on rightfully, a path will be made for you and you will arrive to the other side.

> And so, after he had patiently worked and endured,
> he obtained the promise.
> Hebrews 6.15.KJV

So, you have made it through to the arrival. You've succeeded! There is a moment when you ask yourself, "Did this actually happen?" Have you arrivers ever noticed that sometimes the proud feeling of victory and of reaching your goal doesn't last forever? We are happy for some variable period of time before we set ourselves to do something else. That moment of victory is great. It would last even longer if we truly appreciated the process of arriving. We can get so caught up in the moment that we cannot fully enjoy what's *really* going on. Sometimes we are even blessed when we don't deserve it. Sometimes we are blessed when we don't expect it. Sometimes you can pray without ceasing and initially nothing happens. But, eventually it manifests, and when it does, wow! It feels oh so good! Yes, at first there might have been a bit of denial that overtook you. You might have taken a little time to wonder if it's really happening and not just a dream. But quickly, you begin to find it easier to accept and receive the blessing.

There is a course in making it to the arrival and making the feeling of arriving last. Have you ever noticed how big millionaire lottery winners wait so long in coming forward? I sure have. They can take days after hearing that they've won the millions before they claim their check. Why the delay? What are they waiting for? I'm sure they go through the above process, looking at the numbers over and over again, wondering if it is for real. Eventually, they get everything together to come forward and get the blessing.

> Not that I speak in respect of want: for I have learned,
> in whatsoever state I am, therewith to be content.
> I know both how to be abased, and I know how to abound:
> everywhere and in all things I am instructed both to be full
> and to be hungry, both to abound and to suffer need.
> Philippians 4:11-13.KJV

You've made it now! Take some time and think about your *pathway* to success. Have you learned as the scripture above states, to be content in whatever state you are in? Do you know both how to be full and to be hungry in need? Living that scripture surely makes the arrival that much sweeter! Simultaneously, appreciating the process can keep you steady if God forbid you lose it all. Enjoy your arrival! Stay humble, but celebrate! Stay safe, but celebrate! You made it through the storm. You made it through the love. You made it through the abuse. You made it through the test. You made it through the healing. You made it through the change. You made it through other's opinions. You made it through the interview. You made it through the math. And you made it through the stillness. Yes, you did it! You've arrived in forgiveness. You've arrived in reaching new riches. You've arrived in parenthood. You've arrived in spirituality. You've arrived in waking up to see another beautiful morning. Think about what's to be next in your life. What will be your next arrival? It may be over, but is it *really* over? Did the fat lady sing in your life yet? Look to the next task.

When mountain climbers finally arrive to the top of the mountain, they enjoy the view, reflect on what they went through getting to the top, rest a bit, and then quickly choose another even greater mountain to climb. It's as though arriving to the top of one mountain became the bottom of an even better mountain. You are a mountain climber, too and therefore should keep it moving. Through it all, remember that you have such great things because you are blessed. Not that you are blessed because you have things. Keep climbing to the top! Keep arriving! And, remember that God will see you through!

144

Dr. Jeris Grant is available to speak at conferences, schools and colleges, churches, and other gatherings purposed to encourage young adults and teenagers.

Simply send an email to the following:

Imgoingthrough@live.com

Doctor Grant
(973) 816-1117